HANGING
Daisy

Murder Cruel & Callous

Paul
DIEKELMANN

Copyright © 2014 Paul A. Diekelmann

All rights reserved. No part of this work covered by the copyrights hereon may be reproduced or used in any form or by any means - graphic, electronic, or mechanical, including photocopying, recording, taping, or information storage and retrieval systems - without the prior written permission of the publisher, or, in case of photocopying or other reprographic copying, a license from Access Copyright, the Canadian Copyright Licensing Agency.

Cover Lay-Out by ON TIME Design hkclg@ns.sympatico.ca

Library and Archives Canada Cataloguing in Publication

Diekelmann, Paul,
    Hanging Daisy : murder cruel & callous / Paul Diekelmann.

Includes bibliographical references.
ISBN 978-1-926448-00-8 (pbk.)

    1. Murder--Nova Scotia--Cape Breton Island--History. 2. McEachen, Daisy Delinger, 1884-1957. 3. Morrison, Dan Murdock, 1891-1969. I. Title.

HV6535.C32N65 2014   364.152'3097169   C2014-905099-2

A Boularderie Island Press Publication

boularderieislandpress.com

PRINTED IN CANADA

Dedication

This book is dedicated to the memory of Daisy Delinger McEachen (1884-1957).

My motive was to uncover the truth about why Dan Murdock 'Spinney' Morrison murdered Daisy, a truth that was not revealed at Dan's trial. The facts herein give voice to Daisy's story.

"...whenever you have eliminated the impossible, whatever remains, however improbable, must be the truth."
Sherlock Holmes

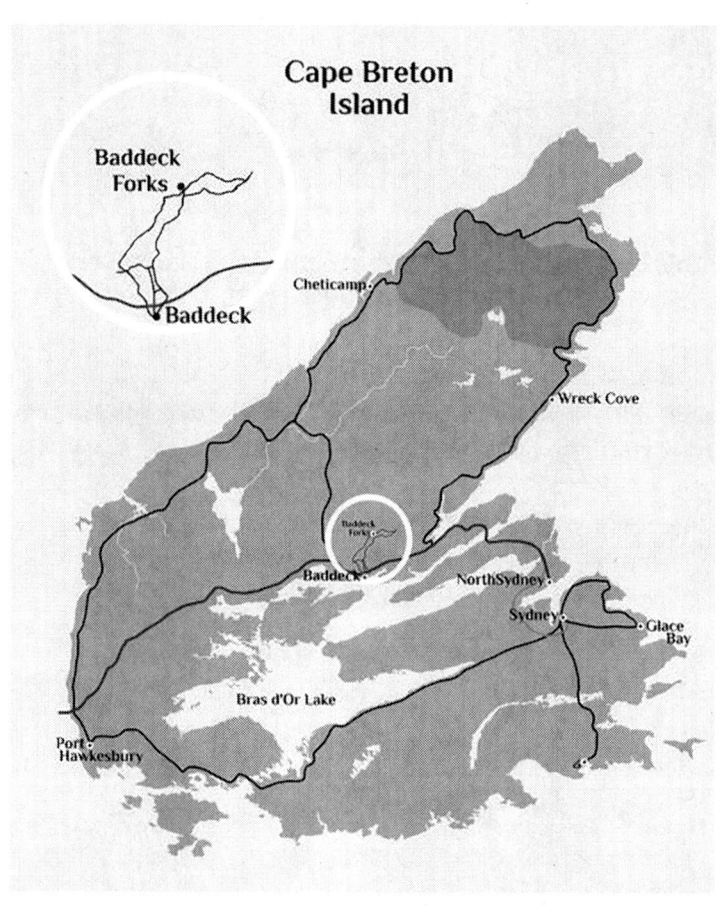

TABLE OF CONTENTS

A Note From The Author..7
Chapter One – *An Unfortunate Alliance*..11
Chapter Two – *Daniel Murdock 'Spinney' Morrison: His Story*.............14
Chapter Three – *Daisy Delinger McEachen*..19
Chapter Four – *Planting Daisy at Baddeck Forks*..27
Chapter Five – *The Battle of Baddeck Forks*...33
Chapter Six – *Dan 'Spinney' Morrison Meets the Loan Arranger*............36
Chapter Seven – *No Good Deed Should Go Unrecorded*.............................42
Chapter Eight – *Daisy Reaches the End of Dan's Rope*..............................44
Chapter Nine – *The Rest of the Story*..55
Epilogue...71
Appendices..76
Appendix A – Daniel Murdock 'Spinney' Morrison's Genealogy......77
Appendix B – Daisy McEachen Genealogy..86
Appendix C – The Trial: Transcripts and Newspaper........................89
Appendix D – The McEachen Family Tragedy....................................123
Appendix E – Attorney John Smith MacIvor, Q.C.,...............................139
Bibliography..144

A Note from the Author

What the mother sings to the cradle goes all the way to the grave.
—Henry Ward Beecher

This is the story of one woman's path from cradle to grave. I hope to grant her justice in the eyes of local history.

Daisy Delinger McEachen Leadley Fisher Morrison (she would assume this long string of names as the years passed) was born in Brooklyn, New York in 1884. She, along with her brother and two sisters were taken by her father and mother to live in Halifax, Nova Scotia in the summer of 1888. The family, in abject poverty, moved to a hovel in Dartmouth in May, 1894. Six months later, the children awoke and found their parents dead.

I have pieced together Daisy's life from the few public records available, her own words as a ten-year-old at the death scene, and some hearsay reports from those who knew her when she lived, many years later, in Whitney Pier (commonly referred to as the Pier) and then at Baddeck Forks, Big Baddeck, Victoria County, Cape Breton Island between 1935 and 1957.

The procedure I have adopted is, in my opinion, the most honest, and thus I have presented material from printed news and government records. Where possible, I have allowed these sources to speak for themselves. When necessary, I have equipped the texts with introductions and explanatory notes from genealogy and archival newspaper records. I have tried to keep my own opinions out of the story. I hope I have succeeded.

The story of *Daniel Murdock 'Spinney' Morrison* and *Daisy Delinger McEachen Leadley Fisher Morrison* is a complicated one shrouded in drama, in rumours, in suspicions and even in lies. Somewhere buried beneath these complexities lies the truth. I have taken it upon myself to present the documented facts and photos I uncovered through years of diligent research, which included the reading and collecting of reports (both written and oral) from a range of sources including local residents, historians, journalists, and eyewitnesses.

I have no personal connection to *Dan* or *Daisy*, though as a youngster growing up in Sydney between 1936 and 1954, I met many adults, and could have made a brief acquaintance with either one of them. For a few months in 1949, when I was 17, I worked as an office boy for J.W.

Stephens. Dan, 57 at the time, worked there during that time; I think I remember him, though I do not recall any specific encounters with him that would pertain to this narrative.

Sometimes people ask me why I became interested in the Morrison murder that occurred in Baddeck Forks, Big Baddeck. What motivated me to probe into the lives of this ill-fated couple?

It is true that I knew nothing of their story until June of 2003, when I stood in the Baddeck Post Office, signing up for a mail box.

Suzanne McDonald, the postal clerk, smiled at me. "Oh! You live in spook hollow!"

I cocked my head to one side. "What do you mean?"

"That's where a man murdered his wife years ago."

This brief exchange was my introduction to the story of Dan and Daisy. Theirs is the only known murder to have occurred in Big Baddeck, Cape Breton Island, Nova Scotia, as of this writing.

The Village Kitchen was a friendly gathering place for Baddeck residents and visitors. My wife Toni and I used to dine there, both for the menu and for conversation with locals. After learning of *Spook Hollow*, I asked two local men to tell me what they knew of its history. Between humorous anecdotes, they shared with me tales that were far from complimentary to the murder victim, Daisy. I began to get the impression that she was a "black widow" villainess, a woman who married older widowers for their money, then did away with them. I also received the impression that Dan was a downtrodden man who was nagged by his wife until he lost his "presence of mind," and killed her.

One of the men, J.P. Asaph (JP) joked, that years after Dan got out of prison, he said of Daisy, "If I knew jail was so good, I would've killed her sooner."

These tales intrigued me. I began to ask older residents of the community about Dan and Daisy. From that time in 2003 until the present day, I have researched these two people, their habits, their early life history, the history of their marriage and life together.

I live in Big Glen, a section of Big Baddeck[1], about a mile from the scene of the murder at Baddeck Forks. I sometimes look out my

---

1   Names of the community can often be confusing. In the early 1800's the heavily populated area was known as Big Glen by the Scottish settlers. Later a section near a fork in the road that led to Baddeck was named Baddeck Forks. The entire landscape around the Baddeck River was/is known as Big Baddeck. The Village of Baddeck was called Little Baddeck. Today the rural area surrounding the Village is known as Big Baddeck. Baddeck Forks is a specific location along the Big Baddeck Road. The Village of Baddeck is the government and business hub of Victoria County.

window and imagine Daisy walking past my home, a route she no doubt took at some point in her life. Daisy became somewhat of an obsession for me because I found it difficult to accept that she was blamed for her own murder. I began to use the phrase, "Daisy walks the Glen;" and now Daisy has walked through my mind for over ten years.

In late October of 2006, near Halloween, a local landscaper, Earl McDonald, who had been working on our property, left his truck and grader parked overnight in our home parking area. My wife Toni and I were in Baddeck at a meeting, while our daughter Pauline remained home alone. As soon as we returned, Pauline told us that the huge grader had started by itself. Not only did we live too far out of the Village and too high up the hilltop for pranksters to trespass, but the grader had no keys in it! Pauline had to call the landscaper to come quickly to bring his keys and turn off the engine.

A few days later while sitting again in The Village Kitchen, I mentioned the grader incident to JP. He shrugged. "Daisy turned it on. She used to drive a tractor."

I'm sure my mouth dropped open. Could he be right?

Since 1991, my wife Toni, our daughter Pauline and I had worked to restore an 1843 farmhouse in Big Glen. Penciled on the wooden plank wall in the hallway are the words Auley G. Morrison, Big Glen. The house had been built and occupied by John and Kenneth Morrison, though research has shown they are probably no relation to Dan. The house is about eleven miles from the Village of Baddeck (known from 1800 to the early 1900s as "Little Baddeck") along the Upper Baddeck River Road at Baddeck Forks. Upper Baddeck had been an early 1800s settlement for many Scottish immigrants. Dan's home was very near Baddeck Forks, about two miles from my home.

My granddaughter Sarah and her friends visited overnight when they were teenagers. I once told them, jokingly of course, that "Daisy walks the Glen." Like many locals, they had heard the villagers' stories about the murder. From that point on, believing Daisy's ghost truly walked through Big Glen, a few of the girls refused to walk up our driveway after dark.

Getting deeper into the lives of Dan and Daisy, I became convinced that their story needed to be shared. Clearing Daisy's reputation was the force driving this search for truth. The day the manuscript was completed I went outside to relax. To my surprise there were huge clusters of daisies growing alongside the patio steps. I had never noticed any daisies growing there before.

Thank you Daisy; they are beautiful.

My thanks go to all who provided information, encouragement, and criticism as the story unfolded: John Campbell for Highlander Newspaper information (and credit should also be offered to his late sister, Anne Marie Campbell for the deep research and writing on the original series of articles in the Highlander); the Beaton Institute and the McConnell Library for copies of documents; Shawna Morrison for her helpful ideas and comments; Ella Fraser for sharing stories and pictures of her Morrison family; Joan MacInnes, Victoria County Archivist, along with many, many others who graciously tolerated my probing questions.

Thanks to my wife Toni, and daughters Pauline, Margaret, and Joanne who patiently listened to the story of Dan and Daisy for more than eight years as I received new information. Those not mentioned here are credited within the book. My thanks go to all of them.

There is a mystery in the story. Why did these two elderly people, Dan and Daisy, marry and remain in the stress-filled relationship for six and a half years until one of them was murdered?

I invite you dear reader to explore this text and determine whether Daisy or Dan—or both—should be blamed as the cause of Daisy's death. Or perhaps there were other forces at work.

You decide.
Paul A. Diekelmann
2014

Chapter One

An Unfortunate Alliance

Daniel and Daisy Morrison[2]

"If we walk with Christ in the daytime,
He will walk with us in the shadows.[3]"

1949 was a year of changes: Canada joined the North Atlantic Treaty Organization (NATO), the USSR detonated a nuclear bomb, and Daniel Murdock 'Spinney' Morrison decided it was time to remarry. Dramatic events, all.

Dan was tired of living alone. A 59-year-old widower familiar with the companionship of a wife and homemaker, Dan decided he needed a companion to prepare meals for him, keep his house clean, and perhaps contribute financially to his bottom line. He'd found fewer and fewer carpentry jobs in Baddeck and surrounding areas, and he brought home less and less money. His house was in need of repair, but he had neither the time, the money, nor the inclination to invest in it.

Perhaps on his own, or perhaps on the advice of a friend, Dan placed an advertisement in a "lonely hearts" column, hoping to find a

---

2   Photograph reprinted with permission. Campbell, Peter A. and Ian Stott. 1981. *Cape Breton Highlander*. Aug. 19, 1981. Killam Library Microfilm Collection, AN 5 C3. Accessed 2013.
3   Quote from a prayer plaque hanging in the kitchen of the Morrison home, as photographed in police records.

suitable wife with whom to live out his years. Of course, it would be helpful if this suitable wife came with a nest egg.

Soon, Daisy Delinger Leadley Fisher responded to Dan's advertisement, touting that she was three years his junior, (though records show she was eight years his senior[4]), her maiden name was Delinger, (Dan and others spelled it 'Dillinger'), and that she'd been left a widow by her late husband, Mr. Albert Fisher, a prosperous Sydney merchant and respected city alderman. She neglected to mention, or else lied by omission, that her birth-name was McEachen, and the puzzle of this exclusion is one I will try solve in the chapters that follow.

Perhaps neither Daisy Fisher nor Dan Morrison knew each other before they became acquainted through the advertisement; however, with Dan's family connections and Daisy's marriage to a city alderman, it is likely they had at least a passing acquaintance in the tightly knit circles of Cape Breton.

When Daisy answered Dan's ad, she was living on Fisher Street at Whitney Pier (also called The Pier), a neighbourhood of Sydney, in a house left to her by her late husband Albert Fisher, who was also an elderly widower (born in 1861) when he married Daisy Delinger Leadley on November 30, 1936. Albert's wife Agnes, born in 1862, passed away in 1934 in Sydney, at age 73, of pneumonia.

Albert had been working as a blacksmith in 1886 when he married Agnes Cox, and the two lived in Stewiacke, Nova Scotia before settling in Whitney Pier. They had had a long and fruitful married life with sons, daughters, and grandchildren—until Agnes's death.

Daisy was only 51 when she married 74-year-old Albert, within a year of Agnes's death. They continued to live at Whitney Pier, and their marriage lasted 10 years, until Albert (age 84) died of age-related medical issues in the hospital at Sydney River on September 6, 1945. These were years when Sydney and the Pier were economically thriving with the steel plant, coal mines, and shipping companies in full production. Jobs, and seemingly money, were plentiful. The Allies had recently won World War II and the future looked bright for Canada and the United States.

Poor women, like Daisy, in the 1800s and early 1900s had few professional opportunities. Many, especially from poor families,

---

4   Genealogy records of the time are filled with birth-year errors, either by recording mistakes, lack of birth records or even by a woman's choice.

sought a career in domestic work that included marriage to an older widower with steady income as a means of livelihood. It was common practice for women to adapt their age, place of birth, nationality, and church affiliation to that desired by the new husband (or employer).

Daisy, born in 1884, was a child of the late 1800's. Her parents had been extremely poor. It was natural, then—perhaps even culturally expected—for Daisy to look for another husband after her prior one died. And one might imagine that Daisy, with her recent inheritance from the Fisher estate, appeared quite an attractive catch to Dan Morrison. The two needed each other.

Daisy began her alliance/relationship with Dan as his housekeeper, though the two soon married. Their summertime wedding took place in 1950, at the Baddeck Forks church. "The marriage of Dan Murdock Morrison and Daisy (Delinger Leadley) Fisher, was anything but romantic," the *Cape Breton Highlander*[5] reported. Daisy had come to her new husband as a housekeeper and companion, not as a romantic lover. She never revealed her true maiden name of McEachen.

Even though romance was not the objective of the marriage, with a mutual goal of support and companionship, what went wrong? Did their separate past histories play a part in the early demise, not only of their convenient marriage, but also of one of the two spouses? Surely there were many marriages of the time built on fewer commonalities and lesser needs, so why did Dan and Daisy's relationship end with one of them swinging by a rope?

---

5   Campbell, Peter A. and Ian Stott. 1981. "This Match Wasn't Made in Heaven," Cape Breton Highlander. Aug. 12, 1981. Killam Library Microfilm Collection, AN 5 C3. Accessed 2013.

Chapter Two

Daniel Murdock 'Spinney' Morrison: His Story

Daniel Murdoch 'Spinney' Morrison was born November 11, 1891 in Big Baddeck, Victoria County, Cape Breton Island to Murdock J. Morrison and Isabella Buchanan. He was a grandson of Donald 'Spinney' Morrison, who was born in 1810, in Strond, Island of Harris, Scotland. Donald had immigrated to Cape Breton and married Christy Shaw, daughter of Alexander Shaw and Sarah Shaw. Christy was born in 1819 in North Gut, Victoria County, Cape Breton. Donald and Christy had eight children; four daughters and four sons. They lived in Big Baddeck, in the area then called Glean Tosh in Gaelic, and known today as Big Glen.

Dan was one of two descendants of Donald 'Spinney' Morrison who continued to carry the 'Spinney' designation in their names. The source of the word spinney is unknown, but might refer to "spinner of wool," just as "Weaver" was a surname or identifier name given to families who were weavers. Some speculate that it is a name for someone who spins stories; in Baddeck Dan was known as 'Spinigan'.

Morrison cousins out west Jack – Dan – Milton (undated)

Dan's grandparents, Donald and Christy, had eight living children who in turn produced sixteen children. Some of these married and gave birth to sons and daughters. Dan lived among this extensive dynamic family and grew up among many brothers, sisters, cousins and in-laws. The boys were jokers, fun-loving and adventurous. Shawna Morrison, a distant relative of Dan's has provided insight into the Baddeck Morrison family dynamics. Shawna, who currently lives in Western Canada, writes:

"My great great grandfather's name was Neil Archibald Morrison, first cousin to Dan Murdock. No family stories were ever mentioned about Dan Murdock Morrison. I do know that my line (Dan's cousins) sound to be very great people...happy, hard workers (mostly farming, grain buying) and Neil Archibald (Murdoch's brother, my uncle) was a CPR supervisor of some sort, helping build the railroad through Manitoba."

Shawna says that "hearing about Dan's habit of joking around a lot...all the Morrison boys that I knew were jokesters and have always loved to laugh. The Morrison boys being Neil's son's line [through] Archibald my great grandfather. He and his sons and daughters were always playing jokes and pranks on each other and people, and making witty comments. Their types of humour have always been ... [similar to] Dan's style of humour. Nobody had ever taken it as mean. Sometimes they see the humour in jokes that are trouble stirring to get a gasping shock as a response...but never had ill or mean intent. In fact, that same type of humour is the Morrison way even today. But nobody ever hurt anyone nor did they ever have any intention to do so. That's not the way they were or are.

Reading about Dan's playfulness, his ways of joking around, does remind me a lot of them. They are and were really liked and loved by a lot of people. No one hated them for it. In fact they all had a lot of friends. I don't know what Archie's siblings and his dad's (Neil) humour was like, though. Our family has always reminisced and laughed about jokes that were played and happenings of the past. Neil's son, Archie, my great grandfather (Milton's brother), was known for his joking around. Sometimes his jokes stirred up trouble, him trying to get a 'rise' out of someone. But everyone who knew his true character knew he was just kidding around and laughed. His boys were the same way, always looking for a laugh. I wonder if the people who really knew and liked Dan back in that day would've said he was mean playing jokes, or are they saying it because he really was mean. Everyone who comes into our lives affects each of us in some ways. He and Daisy obviously never got along and both brought out the worst in each other.[6]"

Dan attended grade school in the Glen at Baddeck Forks, and left with a fourth grade education. Most of these family members, including Dan himself, later moved to Boston and the Northeast United States, Manitoba, Alberta, British Columbia, Saskatchewan and other places

---

6   Email correspondence February 5, 2013 from Shawna Morrison to the author.

where opportunities and jobs were plentiful. Dan grew up with a very large and close family support system.

Dan's father, Murdoch John Morrison, was born in 1859 in Big Glen, Victoria County, Cape Breton, NS. He married Isabella "Bella" Buchanan. They had five children: two sons and three daughters. The 1891 Canadian census shows Murdoch as married and living at home with his parents and a few siblings. One of their sons was Dan Murdock 'Spinney' Morrison.

In 1891, Dan's grandfather Donald was 80 years old, and his grandmother Christy was 71. Murdoch J. Morrison, Dan's father, was 32 years old. Donald had passed away before the 1901 Canadian census. Their sons and daughters grew and moved away to find work better than scraping a hard living from farming the hard soil in Big Baddeck. Some, including Dan moved to the 'Boston States' as it was called by locals.

Murdock J. Morrison   Isabel Buchanan
Dan's parents.

The 1930 US Census shows Daniel M. Morrison, age 38, (born 1892), residing in Claremont, Sullivan County, New Hampshire with his wife, Christine (Tina) Ross-Morrison, 41; ages at marriage are recorded as 37 for Daniel and 41 for Christine. Current records indicate that she was born in French River, Victoria County.

Dan had immigrated to the US in 1925, age 34, and Christine had been in the US since 1913 (year of birth, 1888). Dan's occupation is recorded as "Carpenter working on buildings." There was a great need for skilled workers during this time in the USA. Dan and Tina were married in 1929, and the childless marriage lasted thirteen years, until 1942, when Christine (Tina) died in Boston, where Dan's sister Dollie and Tina's relatives and friends had been living. Dan told the investigating officers in his 1957 statement that Tina died from heart trouble.

Dan and Christine Ross-Morrison

On May 9, 1932 Daniel Murdock Morrison was issued US Naturalization certificate No. 3547972 by the US District Court at Boston, Massachusetts. He was residing at 72 Waverley Street, Boston, Roxbury, Massachusetts. He was 41.

Many people from Nova Scotia, especially the men, immigrated to the USA for work, leaving family and friends behind. The Northeast USA, especially Boston and other large cities, provided thriving centres of employment for carpenters, masons, forgers, farmers, and more. Travel was virtually unimpeded between the two countries, and in those days the Northeastern US was known by Cape Bretoners as 'the Boston States.' Second and third-generation young men descended from the Scottish, Irish, and English first settlers in rural Atlantic Canada surged like rushing waters into the territories of Manitoba, British Columbia, and the early British colonial provinces in North America, where they established themselves and raised families or remained single. They sent money to families at home. Very few, like Daniel Murdock 'Spinney' Morrison, returned to their Cape Breton roots to live permanently.

Nova Scotia had been one of the original fourteen colonies of Great Britain from 1746 until 1820. Many of the early Scottish, British, Irish, and other immigrants who arrived in Halifax in those days knew that they were settling into British territory politically connected to Massachusetts, New Hampshire, and other colonial Provinces in America. This concept remained with their descendants well into the 1800s, even after 13 colonies separated from Britain to form the USA, leaving Nova Scotia the fourteenth and only colony that remained British.

Stocky, soft spoken, well-travelled Dan returned to Cape Breton in the early 1940s as Canada and the world had eyes on WWII. At age 50 he was too old to join the Canadian-British forces so he returned to carpentry, and was a good carpenter according to all reports. He worked for J.W. Stephens Construction Company in Sydney, when there was work to be had. He later worked at the Alexander Graham Bell Museum in Baddeck during its construction in 1953-1954, when things were busy there. During the winter, he cut trees on the farm both for personal firewood and for sale. He hunted game for food in season, and did carpentry jobs for anyone who could pay. Carpentry was his chosen trade since youth. His income was as sporadic as his work habits, but it was enough to support his simple, single-man lifestyle; it was not enough to support both a home and a wife.

Chapter Three

Daisy Delinger McEachen Leadley Fisher Morrison: Her Story

I cannot think of any need in childhood as strong as the need for a father's protection.
— *Sigmund Freud (1856-1939)*

Daisy had an upbringing much different than her husband Dan's. Daisy's childhood was fraught with instability, poverty, and death.

Daisy's father, Charles Alexander Julian McEachen was born on June 6, 1857, in Woolwich, England. Growing up, he went by the name Alexander or Alex most of the time. Alex fancied himself a photographer both before and long after his marriage to Alice Saville in Woolwich, England. Alice Saville, Daisy's mother, was born on September 28, 1853, and married Charles Alexander McEachen in 1878[7].

Alex worked for a while at the Woolwich Royal Ordnance Service, but left employment for an unknown reason. Shortly after marriage, according to Alice's sister-in-law Clara Saville, Alex and Alice were temporarily separated or in trouble of some kind. He wrote her a letter saying his dead body would probably be found in the river Thames if something did not turn up[8].

Alex was one of the unfortunates victimized by the Long Depression (an economic depression resulting in a worldwide recession) in Europe and America. The Long Depression began in 1873 and lasted through the spring of 1879. Though the economic impact was worldwide, it was most severe in Europe and the United States. Until that time, the US experienced steady growth fuelled by the Second Industrial Revolution following the American Civil War.

"In the United States, economists typically refer to the Long Depression as the 'Depression of 1873–79,' kicked off by the Panic of 1873, and followed by the Panic of 1893, book-ending the entire period of the wider Long Depression.[9]" The Long Depression, at sixty-five months in length, out-lasted the Great Depression's forty-three

---
7   Alice's birth date differs on census records. This date was provided by Trudy Baker, a distant cousin of Alice, from family records, by email December 31, 2012, from England.
8   "A Tragic Affair in Dartmouth." Evening Mail October 5, 1894, Halifax, Nova Scotia. Comment to newspaper reporter by Clara Saville, sister-in-law of Alice McEachen.
9   "Long Depression." http://en.wikipedia.org/wiki/Long_Depression.

months of financial heartache.

During this time, Alex McEachen tried to build a career in photography, like thousands of young men in late 1800s Europe and America. In those days, the profession was filled with life-threatening explosives, poisonous chemicals and tremendous competition. Very few succeeded in making a name for themselves as professional photographers. Alex was not among them, but he persisted in striving to be a noted professional. He never succeeded up to the day he died in Dartmouth, Nova Scotia on October 5, 1894.

After Alex's reunion with his wife Alice, their daughter, Alice Maud, was born on July 26, 1879, in Woolwich, England. Unable to find suitable work that he liked, Charles Alexander and Alice immigrated to Brooklyn, NY in 1881. Jobs were said to be plentiful in America. Coney Island, a new entertainment park in Brooklyn, was expanding. New businesses and industries were starting up in New York. Here Alex could use his photography skills, or so he thought. But he still needed money to support Alice and Maud while chasing his dream. During a period from 1881-1882, he worked as a waiter. They lived at 276 Washington Street, Brooklyn, and he found work at Coney Island. In 1886, he was working as some type of inspector.

A son, Alexander (1882), daughter Daisy (1884), and daughter Minnie (1886), were born to Alex and Alice in Brooklyn. The family seemed to be getting along fairly well, until The Great Depression of 1883.

Just when he believed life couldn't get worse, from March 12-14, "The Great Blizzard of 1888" struck the US Northeast. With hurricane-force winds, it dumped thirty to fifty-foot snowdrifts on New York, making work and life impossible for a long time. The very poor, like Alex and his family, suffered the most.

"The Blizzard of 1888;
the Impact of this Devastating Storm on New York Transit"
By G. J. Christiano

When the storm first hit New York City, the temperature was mild as a light rain began to fall on March 11th, gradually increasing in ferocity. By March 12th these torrential rains changed to heavy snow and buried the unprepared city in drifts of up to thirty feet deep!

The temperature plunged and winds reached over eighty miles per hour. This continued for the next 36 hours. Sources vary on the total devastation caused by this massive storm, but over 400 people lost their lives, some 200 in New York City.

This snow storm became legendary, earning the nickname "The Great White Hurricane," after it paralyzed the East Coast from the Chesapeake Bay to Maine. Ships at sea sunk or were grounded, telegraph and telephone wires were down cutting off communication between major cities. All transportation was immobilized. An estimated $25 million was caused in property damage from fires alone. Many cities were hard hit by the blizzard, but New York City was hit hardest of all.

In New York City, by noon on Monday, the snow had fallen to depths of between two to five feet, with drifts piling up over fifteen to thirty feet in many sections of the metropolis.

On Tuesday, the East River was so thoroughly coated with ice that many people were able to walk across from Brooklyn to Manhattan. This was soon stopped by several tugs which chopped up the ice.[10]

After the Great Blizzard of 1888 hit upstate New York Alex, Alice and the children packed their few belongings and moved to Halifax, Nova Scotia. Alice's brother Matthew Harvey Saville (Harvey) had provided substantial financial assistance many times before, and he probably helped again in this instance. Harvey was a foreman at the British Royal Ordnance Service in Halifax. He had been transferred there from Woolwich and supported the British naval and army garrisons in Nova Scotia. Britain was still the Mistress of the Seas, though her glory was fast fading. Halifax had been the gateway for European access to Upper and Western Canada.

In Halifax Alex found work as sexton with the First Baptist Church, Spring Garden Road, where he and his family were given lodging in

---

10 Printed with permission of Gregory Christiano, http://www.nycsubway.org/wiki/The_Blizzard_of_1888%3b_the_Impact_of_this_Devastating_Storm_on_New_York_Transit

the upstairs of the vestry. They remained there until Harvey found work for him at the Ordnance. This lasted for a couple of years.

Unfortunately, Charles Alexander's work hours were changed at the Ordnance, preventing him from doing his church sexton work. Consequently, he quit the good government job and stayed with the church work. In May 1894 he quit the Church and moved to Dartmouth. At this time Alex McEachen was 37 and Alice was 41.

The world-wide economic depression was worsening. One report reads, "The National Bureau of Economic Research estimates that the economic contraction began in January 1893 and continued until June 1894. The economy grew until December 1895, but it was then hit by a second recession that lasted until June 1897.[11]"

Alex had been ill and unemployed for six months while living in Dartmouth, requiring 15- year-old Maud to take charge of selling family clothing and other home items to get money to feed the family. Maud told the police, "Mother has been sick off and on for a long while. The only thing she drank yesterday was a glass of brandy that father gave her. She fainted then. About eleven o'clock in the morning she regained consciousness and said to Daisy, 'Be good.'

She did not speak to Minnie or me. She never spoke again to my knowledge."

Alice was on her way back to bed when she spoke her last words to Daisy, "Be Good;" words that Daisy Delinger McEachen would probably remember for the rest of her life.

Alice died that evening from cyanide poisoning.

When Daisy and her eight-year-old sister Minnie went downstairs the next morning, they found their father, Charles Alexander McEachen, lying dead on the kitchen floor. He had died that morning from cyanide poison.

Photographic chemicals used by photographers of the 19th century were extremely toxic, and the chemicals, including potassium cyanide, were sold without the warning labels or restrictions that now prevent excessive use. Not only were the noxious chemicals hazardous to breathe, but some could be absorbed through the skin, reaching fatal levels in the photographers' bodies. Newspapers of the time reported—almost weekly—the death of another photographer[12].

The deaths of Alex and Alice, however, were not accidental.

---

11   Citation: Whitten, David. "Depression of 1893". EH.Net Encyclopedia, edited by Robert Whaples. August 14, 2001. URL http://eh.net/encyclopedia/article/whitten.panic.189
12   Burgess, J.M. "Photography and Disease." Photographic News. Feb.-May, 1868.

When Alice and Alex moved to Dartmouth in May 1894, Alice was two months pregnant with their fifth child. Potassium cyanide had been for many years used to induce miscarriages and abortions. Under financial pressure and despair, Alex and Alice probably decided they could not handle another child. Alex knew how to administer the tincture of potassium to solve their problem. However, he probably made a mistake; and Alice overdosed on the poison. She lingered for months, growing weaker and weaker. There was no free medical care at the time. No government paid care, no welfare, no child support programs. People were on their own except for some religious societies that tried to help the needy.

The failed abortion attempt put the fear of the law into Alex. Not only was he unemployed, sickly, and broke, but after he and Alice tried to abort her pregnancy, they were now criminals according to Canadian law.

On the morning that Daisy and her siblings found first their deceased mother, then their dead father, they also found a note. On a plain deal table near Alex McEachen's body stood a glass goblet, and beside it lay an oblong piece of white, unruled paper. Written on the paper with blue pencil, in a clear bold hand, was the laconic message:

wife accidentally poisoned.

i cannot stand the loss go to join her.

Alexander administered poison to his wife and then to himself, leaving the four children with neither father nor mother[13].

The suffering and grief that impressionable young Daisy endured in losing both her father and mother in one night is heartbreaking to imagine.

The mother figure was an essential part of the home in nineteenth-century Nova Scotia. The presence and guidance of a mother was a vital part of a girl's childhood, endowing her with socially and domestically appropriate behaviours to equip her for life. Motherless girls had to develop their own ways to understand their role in society. Daisy, very poor and parentless by her early teens, learned to be a domestic servant and homemaker.

After her parents' deaths, Daisy and her brother and sisters lived with their uncle, Harvey Saville. Sometime before age seventeen, she began working for the Lownds Family (spelled Lounds on some records). She cleaned clothes, kept house, cooked, and was available for whatever chores were thrust upon her. She worked for the Lownds

---

13   See Appendix D for newspaper articles on the deaths of Alex and Alice McEachen.

family for ten years, until Mr. Lownds died.

Typically throughout adolescence, a strong current moved young women toward marriage. All of their training pointed them in the direction of managing a home. The reality of women's lives involved opportunism, thrift, and helping wherever necessary; most were adept at making the best of situations.

With limited employment opportunities for women in the 1800s, half were in domestic service. Halifax-Dartmouth during that era was depressing for the underclass, of which Daisy was a member, and it was filled with extreme hardship for women. Some of the jobs available were for seamstresses, washer women, domestic servants, or prostitutes.

Ideally for girls, childhood was a time of beginnings and learning to be a girl. Young womanhood was a time of transition and was spent developing skills and commencing courting practices in preparation for womanhood. Womanhood was the time to put learned skills into effect, fulfilling the role of wife and mother in the warmth of a home. Widowhood was a time of potential freedom, but also of uncertainty, and often dependence. Daisy missed having a childhood that offered these skills.

Remarriage was also common in Nova Scotia in the 1800s, for both widows and widowers. Men remarried more often than women did, and men were considerably more likely to marry younger women. Logic tells us, then, that Daisy was—in some sense—fated to marry multiple widowers.

In England, upon whose laws Canadian law was based, married women had rights similar to the rights of children. That concept filtered into Nova Scotia, a British Colony. Still, the thousands of immigrants from Europe carried with them the idea that the law regarded a married couple as one person. The husband was responsible for his wife and bound by law to protect her. She was supposed to obey him. The husband, even in case of a divorce, then owned the personal property the wife brought into the marriage. The income of the wife belonged completely to her husband, and the custody of children belonged to the father, as well. He was able to refuse any contact between the mother and her children. The wife was not able to conclude a contract on her own. She needed her husband's agreement.

In addition, a married woman could not be punished for certain offences, such as theft or burglary, if she acted under the command of her husband. It was impossible to charge the wife for concealing her husband and for stealing from her husband, as legally they were one person.

Women had no legal say in how many children they would have, nor would they get custody of children if the marriage ended in divorce. However, claims that wives were legally "property" of their husbands are greatly exaggerated. Murder of a wife by her husband was punishable by death, just like the murder of any other person. For a woman to destroy her husband's property was legal. Murder of somebody else's wife was also punishable by death, while destroying his property (i.e., breaking his windows) was a much lesser crime. Beating somebody else's wife was a serious crime, much more serious than damaging a property. In case of disaster or other danger, women (including married women) were supposed to be saved before men, which is also inconsistent with their proposed "property" status.

Daisy was 28 when she married for the first time. Her husband, Frederick William Leadley, was 50 when he took Daisy as his bride on December 12, 1912, only months after the historic sinking of the Titanic. A former blacksmith, Fred was then a labourer at the Acadia Sugar refining company. Fred was born in Windsor, NS, on October 8, 1862 to his father John Leadley and mother Harriet Aikins.

Daisy was not Fred's first wife. True to the social standards of the time, as a widower, he married a woman much younger who was a skilled housekeeper. Fred's first wife, Elizabeth Gates, married him on May 23, 1889. He was 27 at the time, and she was 21. Elizabeth was born in Dartmouth, NS to parents William J. Gates and Elizabeth A. Sharpe. Fred, a brickmaker (a moulder—maker of molds and castings), married his wife in Keene, Cheshire County, New Hampshire.

On the date of Fred and Elizabeth's marriage, Daisy was 5 years old, living in Brooklyn, New York with her parents and siblings.

Though the date of Fred's first wife Elizabeth's death is unknown, the 1911 Canadian census shows Fred as being single and living with his cousin John Anderson and his cousin's family in Woodside, Halifax, NS. At this time Daisy was 27; she married Fred one year later.

Daisy and Fred had one child together, Roy Delinger Leadley.

Fred died on December 2, 1932, at age 71, in Halifax. The cause of his death was heart disease. Daisy's son Roy died of tuberculosis two years later in 1934, at age 20, in Halifax.

We know that Daisy next married the highly respected Sydney businessman, Albert Fisher, who, after his death on September 6, 1945, left her a moderately well-off widow, after ten years of marriage. It is interesting to note that it was also in the Fall of 1945 when Dan negotiated his mortgage for the farm at Baddeck Forks with attorney MacIvor. This was also the same month in which the Japanese surrendered.

After mourning and processing her late husband's estate through probate, Daisy was ready to return to domestic work, a trade that she had first learned and pursued successfully as a young girl in Halifax-Dartmouth. At 66, in 1949, Daisy Delinger McEachen replied to Dan's ad.

Chapter Four

Planting Daisy in Baddeck Forks

The locals of Baddeck Forks were surprised to see stocky, glum-faced Dan's well-dressed, new housekeeper Daisy arrive, carrying an unusual amount of luggage during the muddiest spring they'd remembered. It wasn't only her petite appearance that raised eyebrows—she was well under five feet tall, with grey-streaked red hair and a kind but firm countenance—but the fact that a man as odd as Dan Murdock 'Spinney' Morrison had found a woman who would live with him, even as a housemaid. Dan himself seemed surprised at the manner of Daisy's arrival, and considering the unkempt state of his home when she arrived, he was even more astonished when she stayed. Obviously, she was accustomed to better surroundings than an isolated rural farmhouse.

Daisy took it in stride, however, transplanting herself from city life to farm life at Baddeck Forks. Dan and his house of disrepair became her newest project. After all, it was going to be her house, too, or so she believed, and since she'd been a housekeeper since at least 1901, she excelled in homemaking skills. She relished the challenge and quickly set about making the house into a proper homestead.

Dan, she quickly discovered, had little money or interest to support her efforts. This was, at first, of little concern to Daisy, and she invested her own money into painting and repairing the house. She added new furnishings, including a television set—the first one in Baddeck Forks—and the house soon looked like a home.

Daisy brought more than stylish furnishings to the Morrison home; she also liked to entertain and socialize with the ladies in her new neighbourhood.

Young women and girls from the area visited frequently to enjoy Daisy's lively company and watch the novel television set. She also went to Sydney to visit her old friends and check on her property at The Pier.

Though Dan was used to a well-kept home when he was married for thirteen years prior to 1942 in the United States, he was not used to taking a back seat to a woman who insisted that things should be done her way. Daisy's inheritance money paid for refurbishments to the house, for furnishings, for food and beverages with which she entertained the new onslaught of guests into the home, and therefore she felt some sense of entitlement to how things should be done.

Her first life-changing moment with Dan came when she demanded that he marry her. No longer willing to maintain a subservient position, Daisy firmly insisted that it was improper to live under the same roof with a man without a legal marriage. "...those who knew the couple feel that Daisy forced the marriage and after accepting her ministrations and letting her pay for home improvements, Dan could do naught but comply," reports the *Cape Breton Highlander*[14]. Clearly, Daisy no longer saw herself in the role of mere housekeeper.

Perhaps the reason Daisy felt that her position allowed her certain dominance in the household was because Dan provided little to the family accounts. He'd been a carpenter by trade, but the jobs had become fewer and farther between. He was used to hunting wild game for food and harvesting trees from his acreage. Daisy, who believed Dan to be a widower of some means when she met him, became troubled by his lack of income and began to nag him about his lack of contribution to their living expenses. She believed, rightfully for that time period, that her husband would bring home regular wages, support her in a suitable manner, and that marriage to Dan Morrison would secure her future, both during his life and after his death, when she would inherit his property, financial assets, and cash.

Perhaps because Daisy wanted to keep up appearances, she regularly loaned money to Dan. She had learned shrewd business practices through her late husband's business and financial dealings. Soon she started lending money to his friends, a practice that wasn't always profitable for her.

The couple began to argue. Daisy insisted that Dan hold up his end of the marriage bargain by gaining employment and offering financial support to their household. Between low-paying carpenter jobs, Dan found temporary work as a carpenter during construction of the Alexander Graham Bell Museum in Baddeck, and he began spending more and more nights in town, away from home, rather than commute, as most workers from his region did. He had a relatively active social life, "...taking in the local Ceilidhs and Scotch concerts. He had been active socially too during his years in Boston and later in Sydney.[15]" In

---

[14] Campbell, Peter A. and Ian Stott. 1981. "This Match Wasn't Made in Heaven," Cape Breton Highlander. Aug. 12, 1981. Killam Library Microfilm Collection, AN 5 C3. Accessed 2013.
[15] Campbell, Peter A. and Ian Stott. 1981. "Daisy, Daisy, You're Driving Me Crazy," Cape Breton Highlander. Aug. 19, 1981. Killam Library Microfilm Collection, AN 5 C3. Accessed 2013.

other words, he wasn't bored or lonely while living in town. Besides, return trips to home usually resulted in bickering and arguments that, over time, grew increasingly more hateful.

Reports vary as to Dan's disposition before Daisy entered his life, though most of the townspeople considered him odd. After his marriage to Daisy, however, most of the locals' impressions about Dan converge into one constant: he had a mean streak. His 'Hitler' moustache didn't help his reputation. Stories abound about how Dan sometimes hurtfully pinched the young girls who came to visit Daisy. It is said by women who are now elderly that he played mean tricks on them and scared them. One relative in Western Canada reports that the Morrison men were known for their playful sense of humour and suggests that perhaps Dan's antics were misunderstood by the young girls who favoured Daisy's attention[16].

Short, slender Daisy was well-liked by the girls and women in Baddeck. She maintained a reputation for being helpful, loving, and caring of the elderly and young. Dan, on the other hand, was known to not tell the truth, to withhold information, and try to change the subject or laugh it off when confronted. Daisy was open, honest, and expected people to live up to their responsibilities. Rumours of the time circulated about the couple and their inability to get along. Daisy's frustration level was rising, and the stress was having an ill affect on her health.

The *Cape Breton Highlander* posted this story in a 1981 series on the ill-fated Morrison couple:

> One summer when Dan was supposedly away, Daisy had a neighbour's daughter from the Pier come up and stay with her. The little girl agreed to go only if she could take her litter of newborn kittens with her. Daisy readily agreed, claiming that she loved kittens. But after only a few days at Baddeck, the little girl awoke one morning to a strange keening sound. When she looked out the window to see what was going on, she spied Daisy moaning over the kittens, which she had laid out on a board beside the well. She had drowned the lot of them! When the young visitor protested, Daisy excused

---

16   Shawna Morrison, email message to the author, May 17, 2013. (Shawna Morrison is the great grand-daughter of Archibald Neil Morrison who was first cousin to Dan Murdock "Spinney" Morrison.

the deed by saying that they were underfoot all the time and they had to go. The youngster hot-footed to the next farm where she borrowed pen and paper and wrote her mother an urgent letter asking her to come and bring her home. Even at the tender age of twelve, she sensed something amiss, and was relieved when her mother quickly complied[17].

What is confusing about this story is that Daisy owned a telephone, thus there would have been no need for the girl to write a letter to her mother. However, not every family had a phone in those days and long-distance charges might apply. According to an elderly resident—who wishes to remain unnamed—the truth is that Daisy did not drown the kittens. This woman knew the couple when she was a young girl living nearby. She reports that Dan Murdock drowned the kittens, and insists that Dan had a mean streak that showed itself in teasing cruelty to young girls and animals[18]. From many sources, some cited within this text, Dan was soft-spoken, not known for telling the truth, and he liked to play tricks at others' expense.

One such story is that when Dan ate dinner at a relative's home, their dog often lay under the table waiting for bits of food. Dan would subtly put his foot upon the dog's tail or foot and press down hard until the dog whined, yelped, and scooted from under the table. His cruelty to small animals and children was usually depicted as "just teasing" and was well known.

Sometimes while walking, Dan would cut a switch from a tree branch, and when he came across a young girl walking past, he would "playfully" switch her on the legs in a teasing sort of way. But the girls, now elder women, say it hurt and they did not like it. They were afraid of him. Other times, when some of these same girls were invited by Daisy to come to her home to watch the first TV in the Village, 63-year-old Dan would creep into the room when a mystery story was playing, and suddenly shout, "Boo!" scaring the girls into screaming and crying. No, Dan Murdock 'Spinney' Morrison was not beloved by the young girls and women of Baddeck. This, of course, led to more arguments between Dan and Daisy.

---

17 Campbell, Peter A. and Ian Stott. 1981. "This Match Wasn't Made in Heaven," Cape Breton Highlander. Aug. 12, 1981. Killam Library Microfilm Collection, AN 5 C3. Accessed 2013.
18 Name withheld by request. Personal interview with the author. February, 15 2013.

Only two years after the wedding, the couple's arguing reached such a point that Daisy took Dan to court for non-support. Though the customs of the time demanded Dan support her, the fact that she'd dragged him into court was a serious embarrassment to Dan. He was, in his opinion, a very hard-working man. He had been a member in good standing of the Baddeck Masonic Lodge, and it mortified him to have his good name dragged through the muck by his wife, in front of his peers. After all, Dan still took care of Daisy in ways other than financially.

The *Cape Breton Highlander* reported in their August 1981 series on the couple that, "In a letter to a friend in Sydney in 1956, Daisy said, 'Dan got through working at the Museum, he was home for three weeks, now he is working on a small job in Baddeck, while home, he shot a large deer, we gave a lot away, but I still have a lot to eat yet. Dan got me a lot of coal and he chopped a winter's kindling wood for me...[19]'"

Dan believed he was a supportive husband. What did Daisy lack? She had a beautiful home she had decorated to her own suiting. She had friends from Sydney who visited her regularly. She even owned a car, which she often hired a local boy, Junior McKay, to drive, taking her to visit her friends in Sydney, most of whom were her former tenants.

However, when Daisy took Dan to court, she was only doing what any good, hard-working, caring and dedicated wife would do under similar stressful circumstances. Dan's financial participation in household expenses was insignificant, a fact he cared nothing about. During the two years they'd been married, Daisy had watched her finances steadily dwindle as she first repaired, then furnished his home, then spent more of her own money to provide upkeep, including food, toiletries, and household items. Dan showed her no real interest in paying back the money she'd loaned him, or even contributing his fair share to their household accounts.

Dan didn't care. He had never asked her to repair or furnish the home. In fact, it is likely that he didn't even legally own the house—a fact he'd never shared with Daisy. She had her own money—enough to loan to his friends, even—so why should she ask for his?

After the embarrassment of court, Dan spent even less time at

---

19 Campbell, Peter A. and Ian Stott. 1981. "This Match Wasn't Made in Heaven," Cape Breton Highlander. Aug. 12, 1981. Killam Library Microfilm Collection, AN 5 C3. Accessed 2013.

home. If he wasn't living there, why should he contribute money to household expenses? He continued to work odd carpentry jobs in town, cut timber, and hunt game. In short, he largely returned to the lifestyle he was used to living before Daisy came into his life.

When he did return home, the arguments became more than heated—they became threatening and even violent.

Chapter Five

The Battle of Baddeck Forks

During Dan's increasing number of absences, Daisy became lonely and perhaps even angrier. When Dan would return home, the bickering quickly escalated into arguing, with shouting so loud that the neighbours, who lived a good distance away, could hear the ruckus. The couple's arguments and bitter quarrels were well known by the residents of Baddeck. At community gatherings, Daisy often criticized her husband in public.

A former neighbour said that sometimes she heard gunshots from the vicinity of the Morrison property, and during those times, her father commented, "I hope he hasn't killed her." He sometimes left their house to go over to the Morrison's to see if everything was all right.

Old-time residents in Baddeck who knew the couple had many stories to tell about Dan's attempts to kill his wife or scare her into leaving permanently. It is said by a few, however, that some of the tales were spread by Daisy herself.

One tale says that Dan borrowed a chainsaw from a friend. When Daisy was asleep upstairs that night, he went into her room planning to kill her with the saw. Fortunately, the saw would not start.

Another time, Daisy told friends that 'Spinney' had balanced a heavy object on top of her new refrigerator, so that when little Daisy opened the fridge door, the object would fall on her head, and hurt — or even kill her.

There is one story in which Dan told Daisy he was going to visit his sister, Dollie, in Boston. He left for a few days and quietly crept back to the house, went into the woods behind the outhouse with his rifle and waited for her to go to the toilet. Now the outhouse had two compartments, one for him and one for her. When Dan saw Daisy entering the outhouse, he waited until she settled and then shot into the back of her stall. He then slipped away and returned home a few days later.

Upon entering his home, he was surprised to find Daisy still alive. Later he realized that he had fired into her side of the outhouse, but she had been using his side.

While this story may indeed be a tall tale, there is valid reason to believe it could also be true. In an interview with Linda MacLean Hirsch, she states that her aunt and uncle knew Dan and Daisy and told Linda many years later that, "...Dan used to take shots at Daisy when she was in the outhouse and in the house..." This triggered Linda to remember that, "...as kids, we actually saw the .22 calibre bullet holes in the back of the outhouse. Now, whether they were from him shooting at her, or just someone target practicing, I cannot say.[20]"

Another story is that Dan took Daisy into the woods one day when he went to cut trees. She was to clean up the twigs, branches and other debris. He positioned her work area under the tree he was cutting and hoped to have the large tree "accidentally" fall upon her. The tree fell, but Daisy escaped injury, because the tree hung up on another tree without reaching the ground where Daisy had been working.

We must remember that at this point, Dan was in his early sixties. He'd worked hard (when he'd worked), doing back-breaking labour with his hands: carpentry, logging, and other manual labour. He was wearing down. When hard-working men return home, they want rest and peace, not another argument over money they don't have. This was especially true for Dan, whose wife appeared to have plenty of money.

Daisy had inherited over 16,000 dollars and a home at Whitney Pier from her late husband, Albert Fisher. When she moved in with Dan she also had monthly income from the sale of her Pier home. We can surmise that she likely inherited property and/or money from her first husband, Frederick Leadley, as well. While 16,000 dollars wasn't considered a landslide of money in the 1940s and '50s, it was enough— at least added to what she already might have had from the Leadley estate— "to afford her a new car every year or so, as well as the fur coats she sported around town," according to rumour[21].

Still, Daisy was accustomed to this lifestyle. She had been a remarkably fine housekeeper, first with the Lownds family for ten years from age seventeen, in Halifax, then as homemaker for her first two husbands: twenty years with Fred Leadley, and ten years with Albert Fisher. She had also been a loving mother for twenty years until her son, Roy William Delinger Leadley died of tuberculosis in Halifax on August 27, 1934. Her husbands had shown their appreciation for her hard-working contribution to their home life by offering financial

---

20   Hirsch, Linda MacLean, email message to the author, February 15 2013.
21   *Cape Breton Highlander*

support and emotional security—as well as a nice inheritance upon their deaths. She showed this same work ethic in the Morrison home by doing laundry, cooking, cleaning, entertaining and keeping the home well-furnished and in good repair inside and out. Did she deserve to be treated with any less respect and less support from Dan? She didn't think so.

But if Daisy felt Dan was taking advantage of her, why didn't she leave? That answer is a simple one. Daisy had, by now, invested quite a bit of money into the Morrison home. It had gone from little more than a hovel in disrepair to a fine home, worthy of socialite visitors. It bore evidence of the stylish touch of a woman of taste, full of furnishings paid for by her own hand. She had every reason to consider it her asset, by right of matrimony, and she believed it would belong solely to her after her husband's demise. No, Daisy wasn't leaving. She was staying, and she continued to hound Dan for financial support. She might also have been pushing Dan to show her the legally recorded deed for the home and property, which he was never able to produce for her or anyone else.

Staying away from Daisy was indeed easier on Dan's nerves. In a statement, Dan Murdock told the police that, "According to her, her first husband was a saint and Dan Murdock could never measure up to that standard.[22]"

There were also rumours, perhaps spread by Dan, himself, that Daisy had pushed her first husband, Fred Leadley, out of a horse-drawn wagon, and that this was the cause of his demise. In fact, Nova Scotia Genealogy archives show that this is, indeed, only a rumour, entirely false. Daisy and Frederick were married for twenty years, until 71- year-old Frederick was hospitalized on October 20, 1932, in Halifax. He died in hospital on December 2, 1932. Cause of death is listed as valvular disease of heart[23].

Daisy did not kill her late spouse.

Unfortunately, in days to come, Dan would not be able to say the same.

---

22   Campbell, Peter A. and Ian Stott. 1981. "Daisy, Daisy, You're Driving Me Crazy," Cape Breton Highlander. Aug. 19, 1981. Killam Library Microfilm Collection, AN 5 C3. Accessed 2013.
23   www.NovaScotiaGenealogy.ca

Chapter Six

Dan 'Spinney' Morrison Meets the Loan Arranger

Home, Sweet Home
The Morrison Home, August 9, 2010
Upper Big Baddeck Road, Baddeck Forks, Baddeck, Cape Breton Island, NS
The house was demolished in 2010.
May God's Eye rest upon this home, day and night[24].

Front view. Dan's niece Ella May Oakley (left) and Ella's grandson Jonathan MacLeod

---

24 Quote from a prayer plaque hanging in the kitchen of the Morrison home, as photographed in police records.

After his first wife Christine (Tina) Ross-Morrison died of heart trouble in 1942 in Boston, 51-year-old Dan Murdock 'Spinney' Morrison returned to Cape Breton. He'd heard that the MacLeod property was for sale near his childhood home at Baddeck Forks, and he wanted to inquire about its purchase. Dan met with Attorney John (J) Smith MacIvor and on December 20, 1945, when Mr. MacIvor was successfully pursuing Provincial election, they signed a mortgage agreement for 800 dollars, plus 5 percent interest.

The mortgagee was John Smith MacIvor for the MacLeod Trust. The terms of the mortgage required that Dan pay the purchase price on the following schedule: 400 dollars, plus 5 percent interest on or before the first day of July, 1946, and the balance and interest to be paid on or before December 20, 1946. The mortgage allowed for the house and property to be reclaimed by the mortgagee (MacIvor) in case of default. Dan was required to pay the taxes, keep the property insured for 800 dollars against fire, and deposit the policies and receipts with the Mortgagee (Attorney MacIvor), and pay all taxes and charges against the property.

According to Victoria County archivist Joan MacInnes, "The Farm consisted of about 200 acres and a beautiful home. The house was built around 1860 in the vernacular style. It was a one-and-a-half-storey wood construction, with a steep gable roof, return eaves, corner boards with cornice, and barge boards. There was one off-centre brick chimney. The windows are double-hung (2/2). The exterior cladding is wooden clapboards. There are pediment pointed dormers, centrally situated on the front and rear elevations. They are three-sided and have scalloped shingles. The front façade is triple-bay—symmetrical. There is a gable-roofed, enclosed entry porch on the front. The foundation is fieldstone. There is a small gable-roofed, enclosed porch on the western end of the house.[25]"

Further description of the house at the time of Daisy's death reveals that, "As you enter there was a small porch, a large kitchen, and off the kitchen was a bedroom, and to the right as you walked into the kitchen there was doorway leading to the front hall and a bit of a pantry to the left. On the right side of the hall was a dining room, and to the left was a sitting room and a storeroom behind that. The stairs were in the hall that went to the second floor. As you proceeded upstairs there were

---

25   McInnes, Joan. Victoria County Archivist, June 16, 1990.

two rooms on the right and two on the left.[26]"

A lovely home, no doubt, especially when refined according to Daisy's standards. Dan moved into his new home and settled into his childhood neighbourhood where he lived quietly, happily and frugally, until August 1950. It was then that he married a widow whom he knew as Daisy Delinger Leadley Fisher. During interviews with the RCMP investigators on February 2, 1957, Dan Murdock said, "The farm is in my name and I look after it and keep the house going."[27] In truth, he had been the registered occupant (not deeded owner) of the property, as evidenced on county tax records. The record does show that he was the person to whom tax notices were handed by the municipal tax agent; however, recorded ownership remained with Attorney MacIvor from 1943 to August 1957. Dan might have thought he was the owner, but he was not the owner on the county tax registry at the time he made the murder scene statement to police on February 2, 1957, while his wife Daisy was hanging dead in the hallway of the home she had cared for.

The house was originally built and owned by farmer and carpenter, Norman MacLeod in 1854. He lived in it until his death in 1903, when his son Roderick A. MacLeod inherited it. Like his father, Roderick was a carpenter. He lived in the home forty years until he died in 1943. His will, dated October 9, 1940, was recorded on January 6, 1941. In his will, Roderick left his estate in trust with Executor Attorney John (J.) Smith MacIvor, Q.C. Roderick had made provision in the will for sale of his possessions and distribution of the money[28]. He had never married and had no heirs. The proceeds from sale of his property were left to the Baddeck Forks cemetery, the Presbyterian College in Montreal, and to pay death and burial expenses.

Here is an excerpt from Roderick's handwritten will:

> "I hereby direct that all my Just debts, funeral and testamentary expenses be paid by my barrister as soon as convenient after my demise.
>
> "I do hereby designate and appoint J. Smith MacIvor, of North Sydney, in the County of Cape Breton...to be

---

26   Duff, A.L., The Trial of Dan Murdock Morrison," 1957. (A.L. Duff was a Corporal of the Baddeck RCMP Detachment who testified in Dan's trial.)
27   Dan Murdock Morrison statement (C-1) to RCMP investigator Corporal Duff, February 2nd 1957.
28   MacLeod, Roderick Angus. "Last Will and Testament," October 1, 1940. (Handwritten)

Executor and Trustee of this, my last will and testament.

"I do give, Devise and Bequeath unto my said Executor all the property, both real and personal of which I may die possessed, with all powers of sale...and deal with the same as follows:

to pay to the Trustees, Committees in charge, or Directors of the Corporation, of the Cemetery at Baddeck Forks … the sum of three hundred dollars ($300). My said Executor being hereby directed to pay no more than fifty dollars ($50.00) in any one year in this regard...for keeping and improving the said cemetery...until the full amount is completely paid...

To pay the income from all the rest and residue each year to the Principal of the Presbyterian College at Montreal to be applied by him in the expenses, needs and tuition fees of such student of the Ministry of the Presbyterian Church in Canada from the said County of Victoria, as in the discretion of the said Principal seems most deserving... (instruction for the distribution follow[29]).

It is my intention that my said Barrister shall dispose of my real property as soon as possible after my death and invest the proceeds received from the sale of...farm equipment...and all other personal property with monies in bank...to be invested in government securities...[30]"

The mortgage signed by Daniel Murdock Morrison and Attorney MacIvor in 1945 had a provision for the property to be redeemed if the 800-dollar sale price, plus interest, was not paid in full by December 20, 1946.

Roderick Angus MacLeod's bequest to the Presbyterian College in Montreal was not paid until 1957. This appears to affirm that the mortgage payments had been 'overlooked' for twelve years. Dan was definitely not the deeded owner of the Roderick MacLeod property while living in the house and married to Daisy. Could this be one

---

29   Page 320-321 of the A&P 1958, within the "Report of the Board of the Presbyterian College, Montreal, 1957-58" says: "A number of friends have remembered the College again this year, and it is with deep appreciation that we acknowledge the following gifts... Roderick Angus MacLeod Estate, twelve thousand dollars, the revenue of which to assist students from Victoria County in Cape Breton."
30   MacLeod, Roderick Angus. "Last Will and Testament," October 1, 1940. (Handwritten)

reason that Daisy was so belligerent with Dan?

We will soon examine how, on June 1, 1957, Dan was sentenced to death by hanging for the murder of his wife Daisy Delinger Morrison. According to local lore the gallows was being built behind the Victoria County Courthouse shortly after the sentence was pronounced. Attorney J. Smith MacIvor, QC, who had arranged the 800-dollar mortgage of the MacLeod property to Dan way back in 1945, inconveniently died eleven days later, at age 44, from coronary thrombosis, on June 12, 1957. He had been ill since at least 1947, but had been more than able to handle his onerous Provincial political duties as well as continue law practice following his defeat in the election of 1956. He resumed his law practice in late 1956. On February 18, 1957, the December 20, 1945 Mortgage indenture between him and Daniel Murdock Morrison was registered with Victoria County.

Upon Mr. MacIvor's death, his Will, dated 17 April, 1957, appointed attorney Donald N. Nicholson his sole Executor and Trustee. Mr. Nicholson determined that there was no record showing the 1945 mortgage had been paid. When Dan was asked about the mortgage he said that he lost the paperwork. Based upon that statement on August 13, 1957, Mr. Nicholson immediately began the legal process to correct the situation due to the "lost paperwork."

At this time, the house and property was unoccupied and still legally owned by John Smith MacIvor in Trust. Dan was in jail waiting to be hanged on 21 August, 1957 for the murder of his wife Daisy. Mr. Nicholson prepared legal documents to: 1. Acknowledge that Daniel Murdock Morrison had paid $1500 for the described property and had asked for a new Deed (Doc. 17770); 2. Quit claim the property to Daniel Morrison assuring that the 1945 mortgage of $800 principal plus interest had been paid off (Doc. 17778); 3. Quit claim the property from Dan Morrison to a third party buyer (Doc. 17777).

Coincidently, 5 percent interest on $800 unpaid for twelve years (1945-1957) is $1436.69.

This pile of stone, metal, and burnt wood are the remains of the Morrison home on Big Baddeck Road, at Baddeck Forks.
(October 2010)

Dirt road below the Morrison home, where police vehicles parked in 1957, during the investigation.

Driveway leading to the Morrison home.

Chapter Seven

No Good Deed Should Go Unrecorded

Like a kettle of water placed over the heat, the relationship between Dan and Daisy Morrison soon boiled dry, and there was nothing left but a blazing fire. Daisy became increasingly more anxious, fearful, and frustrated with Dan's disinterest in supporting her and paying for his home maintenance, food, and general expenses; and he seldom repaid his loans. She certainly must have searched the house for Dan's home ownership documents. Dan, on the other hand, grew evermore frustrated with Daisy's nagging, and stayed away from home more and more.

Once in a great while, Dan would invite Daisy to a local gathering, but this typically resulted in Daisy publicly criticizing him and speaking harshly to him. He began to exclude her from accompanying him, and Daisy was hurt by this exclusion.

Former friends stood on the sidelines and watched, gradually shunning Daisy more and more. She found herself increasingly dependent upon Dan for the moral, emotional and material support that he was unable or unwilling to provide. This situation did not suit either of them and matters grew steadily worse, until they reached rock-bottom on February 2, 1957.

At this time Dan was 66, and Daisy was 73.

Dan's struggle to find work became even more difficult, perhaps because of his advancing age. He was still able-bodied, however, and during one particular week in the winter of '56, he cut five cords of pulp in a single week, by his own hand.

On a typical day, Dan would wake and scavenge the kitchen for breakfast (Daisy, obsessed with her dwindling funds and Dan's lack of monetary contribution, now locked away the food she purchased) and then he headed to the woods around eight in the morning. He would work felling trees and chopping wood until returning home around one o'clock in the afternoon for dinner. Of course, another argument between Daisy and him would ensue, and Dan would hastily eat and then return to the woods until suppertime.

After supper, it was Dan's habit to lie down for a rest, but, as the *Cape Breton Highlander* reported, "Daisy spoiled this on him too with her railing and ranting, he told the police. And when he wanted to retire early for the night, she seemed to come to life, screaming and yelling and using abusive language on him.[31]"

Dan neither understood nor cared about Daisy's fears for financial survival. Daisy did not understand Dan's uncaring attitude about her and the house. And Daisy was beginning to have health problems. She had severe headaches and often became quite nervous and upset, usually due to her financial stressors. Where was the registered deed that proved Dan owned the property? She couldn't find it and he wouldn't talk about it, other than to say that he lost it.

This downward spiral, perhaps influenced by the usual isolation and depression of a frigid winter, increased in speed and vortex until the early morning of February 2, 1957, when Dan finally exploded.

Alex MacLean, one of Dan's friends who'd known him about thirty years, received a phone call from an extremely agitated Dan around 1:15 in the afternoon, summoning him urgently to the Morrison home. Alex wasted no time asking for details, but rather left immediately to cover the one-mile distance between his home and the Morrison farm.

"When I got there he was standing alone outside at the door of his house. No one else was present. I asked him what was wrong. He said, 'Daisy hung herself.[32]'"

Police photo published in *Cape Breton Highlander* showing upset chair in hallway of Morrison household.

---

31   Campbell, Peter A. and Ian Stott. 1981. "Daisy, Daisy, You're Driving Me Crazy," Cape Breton Highlander, August 19, 1981. Killam Library Microfilm Collection, AN 5 C3. Accessed 2013.
32   Excerpted from testimony during the murder trial of Dan Murdock Morrison, May 28-June 1, 1957. See Appendix D.

Chapter Eight

Daisy Reaches the End of Dan's Rope[33]

Dan led his friend and neighbour, Alex MacLean, through the kitchen door, into the house. Alex must have been shocked to see tiny Daisy dangling at the end of a rope, her feet several inches from the floor. A few feet away, a chair lay overturned on the floor.

"What should I do?" Dan asked.

Alex thought for a moment. "The best thing to do is to call the doctor."

While Dan made the call to Dr. C. L. MacMillan, Alex made the twenty-minute drive to the home of neighbours Mr. and Mrs. Dan Neil MacMillan, to share the horrific news with them. Twenty minutes later, he and the couple headed back toward the Morrison home.

When they arrived, Dan and Dr. MacMillan were walking together up the long driveway toward the Morrison home, where Daisy was still hanging. Dan had walked down the drive to meet the doctor. Dr. MacMillan had known Dan for several years, but he did not know Daisy quite as well. She had been to his office only once.

Dr. MacMillan accompanied Dan the three hundred yards up the hill to the farmhouse, and the going was slow because of the considerable snow. He questioned Dan about Daisy's mental condition and mental health. Dan explained that Daisy had not been well, and he said he was coaxing her to go to see a doctor, but she refused. He said that when he came home the night before, she told him she took a dizzy spell and fell. Dan also told the doctor that he'd been working that morning in the woods, cutting firewood, and when he came home, he found the door locked and no dinner ready. He said he thought Daisy was upstairs, but when he opened the door, he found her hanging in the hall. "When he told me she had hung herself, the first thing that came to mind was to ask him about her mental health," Dr. MacMillan said. "Generally something is wrong with a person when they hang themselves.[34]"

It was about that time when Alex MacLean caught up to the doctor and Dan Morrison.

---

33 Author's Note: The story told in this chapter is truthfully relayed from the transcripts of Dan Murdock Morrison's trial, as well as from recent testimony of an eyewitness. Excerpts from the actual trial transcripts can be found in Appendix D, at the end of this book.

34 Dr. C.J. MacMillan testimony at Dan Morrison trial

"When I got there, Dr. MacMillan asked me if I would go back to the road and stop the RCMP, and I did," Alex MacLean said[35]. Knowing police were on the way, and likely not wanting to be involved in what he now realized must be a criminal investigation, Alex took Dan Neil MacMillan and his wife back to their home, and then he returned to his own home.

When Dr. MacMillan examined the body, he found evidence of rigor mortis around the eyes and jaws and hands. Rigor mortis had not set throughout the rest of the body, therefore the doctor determined Daisy had died three or four hours earlier.

Corporal A.L. Duff, an acquaintance of Dan Morrison, was a fifteen-year veteran of the RCMP who had been stationed in Baddeck for the past four and a half years, prior to Daisy's death. Cpl. Duff was the first officer to arrive on the scene. He entered through the kitchen where Dan was sitting in a rocking chair to the left of the stove. He was shown to the front hall where he found Daisy hanging from a new hemp rope tied to the stairway banister in the hallway of the Morrison home. One of Daisy's slippers lay near an overturned chair, a few feet away from her one bare foot.

"I noticed the rope from which she was suspended had stains which appeared to be blood," Duff reported, "and considerable blood matted her hair. There was a cut on the left temple of the deceased, which I presumed had caused the blood in her hair. Her hands were clean. No sign of blood on them. She was fully clothed."

Cpl. Duff also noticed a significant amount of blood on the back of Daisy's neck, though there was none on the front. He also spotted bloodstains on the floor, the wall and on the stair treads leading up the steps to where the rope was tied with a double half-hitch knot.

When Cpl. Duff interviewed Dan Morrison, Dan told him Daisy suffered from severe headaches, usually because she became nervous and upset over her financial condition. During the interview, Cpl. Duff noted the bloodstains on Dan's clothing.

It was then that the Corporal excused himself to return to his car, where he called for back-up. Twenty minutes later, he addressed Dan Morrison. "You need not say anything. You have nothing to hope from any promise of favour; nothing to fear from any threat whether or not you say anything. Anything you do and say may be used as evidence against you." Then Cpl. Duff began to take a statement from Dan

---

35   Alex MacLean testimony at trial.

Morrison. Duff would ask questions and Dan would give answers. Duff would write the answers down and read them back and ask him if they were correct. When Dan stated they were, Cpl. Duff would continue questions until the statement was completed. Corporal Duff told the Court "I then read the statement over and asked him if there were changes he wished to make." This statement is marked C/1 in the Trial Transcript. It was the first statement by Dan, taken on the day of Daisy's hanging. The statement follows:

Statement C/1 evidence. Feb. 2nd, 1957
Statement of Daniel Murdock Morrison Baddeck Forks, N.S.

I have been warned by Corporal Duff that I need not say anything. I have nothing to hope from any promise or favour, and nothing to fear from any threat whether or not I say anything, anything I do say may be used as evidence.

I am a married man and have been living with my wife at Baddeck Forks off and on for the past six years. I am 68 years of age and my wife is about four years younger than I am. Her name was Daisy Morrison. She had been previously married to a man by the name of Fisher who lived at the Pier in Sydney. Her maiden name was Dillinger and had been brought up in Halifax, N.S.

My wife and I were married in the month of August 1950 and she lived at Baddeck ever since. I have worked away quite a bit and last winter I worked in Baddeck until the month of October and then did a few jobs around until December 1956 when I returned home and started cutting pulp. I have been cutting pulp alone for the past week or so off and on and I have cut about five cord. My wife has been living at home all the time except when she would go for a visit to Sydney, N.S. She had no relatives that she knew of but visited friends in the Pier District. She had a house in Sydney that she was selling and having a bit of trouble getting her monthly payments.

Since the last two years she has had headaches and she wouldn't go to the doctor. She became very nervous and would get upset over little things. She had loned [sic] a hundred dollars to Murdock MacKay and she was worried that she wouldn't get it back. She also loned [sic] money to someone else but I don't know who it was, and all this bothered her.

She told me on several occasions that some time I would come home and she wouldn't be living and I was not to worry about her. It seemed that it was always over money that she seemed to get upset. I didn't think that she would ever do anything to herself as she talked about it so much.

I went to the woods this morning about 8:15 A.M. this date and I told her when I left that I wouldn't be home until 1 P.M. I returned about 1:15 P.M. and when I got to the back door I found the door locked. I had a key and I opened the door and walked in. When I walked into the kitchen I noticed it was cold and I called to my wife. There was no answer and I started into the hall and found my wife hanging from the staircase. I did not touch her but went to the phone and called Alexander MacLean my neighbour and he came over. He came over and then I called the doctor and the police came out. At no time did I touch or remove the remains. They are just as I found them. My wife and I always got along well and always had enough to live on. I have made pretty good money the last few years out working and this is only the second month home from working out.

I was married before and my first wife died in 1943 in the U.S.A. with a heart condition. I have no children.

I know nothing of my wife's business transactions as she was very independent and didn't want anyone to know about her business I don't know how much money she had and I don't know anything about the house she was selling.

The farm is in my name and I look after it and keep the house going. My wife was always good to get the meals on time but today when I got home there was no dinner ready. We always got along well and never had any trouble between us or any quarrels. This is a true

statement to the best of my knowledge.
WITNESS – A.L. DUFF Signed – Dan M. MORRISON

After signing statement C/1, about 6:00 P.M., Dan made tea and he and Corporal Duff each had a cup. Shortly after 6:00 P.M., other officers arrived on the scene: Constable Tiller and Constable Brooks, Sergeant Finney and Constable Roger Haddad, who, to this day, cannot forget the terrible scene[36].

"The crime scene was very vivid in my mind. I saw a small grey-haired woman hanging from a rope, her head to one side and slightly bent down and pale in the face. The rope around her neck was attached to the overhead banister, with her feet clear of the floor."

Constable Roger Haddad, then a three year member of the RCMP, was not part of the investigative team. He had been assigned to drive Constable Chris Tiller, the Identification member of the team, with his equipment, from Sydney to the scene at Baddeck Forks.

He said, "We walked from the snow-covered gravel road up to the old farmhouse. I never saw any livestock, sleigh or wagon. Tiller had taken many photos with the flash camera of the total downstairs area: kitchen, hallway, and stairwell and beyond. I had assisted him with measurements. Tiller dusted different areas at the scene for fingerprints. I noted the kitchen wood stove, wooden table and chairs, and an iron skillet on the wood stove. A closed porch led to the kitchen. There was no heat in the building at the time."

The team began collecting evidence from inside and outside the house. After they were finished and preparing to leave, Sergeant Finney asked Dan if he would like to come to Baddeck or stay in his own home and he said he would sooner come to Baddeck. He was not under arrest at this time. Sergeant Finney took him to the RCMP Detachment in Baddeck where they had a short conversation. Dan said he had no money to pay for lodging. Finney suggested he might get Dan lodging in the County jail. Dan said that would suit him just fine. So Sergeant Finney arranged with the jailer to give Dan lodging for the night.

Constable Roger Haddad said, "That evening I stood guard for a couple of hours while Morrison was in an unlocked cell. He kept rambling on about what happened. I repeated the police warning to him that what he said could be used in court. Morrison said, 'When

---

36   Haddad, Roger retired RCMP from emails to author 18 May 2013 – 27 July 2013

she called me a whore's bastard that is when I lost my temper and struck her with the skillet on the head.' While he kept rambling on I told him to keep quiet." Constable Haddad was due to transfer to a new assignment in another Province and therefore was not one of the investigative team on this case. He had not been called to testify in Court.

Daisy's body was removed from the home that evening and Sydney physician and pathologist, Dr. Gyorfi, performed an autopsy from 10:00 A.M. to noon, on February 3 at Victoria County Memorial Hospital in Baddeck.

The doctor found a sharp-edged, superficial cut over the left temporal area about one inch above the left eyebrow, dried blood over the temporal area and in Daisy's hair, but not on any other part of her face. This showed that the body was in a horizontal position when bleeding occurred; otherwise, it would have run over the face.

Dr. Gyorfi reported the usual autopsy details that follow most hangings (swollen tongue that's protruding and bitten, a furrow around the neck, swollen legs due to blood pooling in the lower extremities), but there were other signs, as well, which didn't pertain to death by hanging.

Daisy had rib fractures on both sides; the 5th, 6th, 7th, 8th, 9th, 10th and 11th ribs were parted on both sides—seven broken ribs on each side. The fractures were in a straight line, each rib symmetrically broken above the other at about the same level. Blood had settled around the fractures between the breastbone and the skin. The lower part of both the left and right lungs was congested with blood. Extensive haemorrhaging had taken place in the abdomen, between the peritoneum (which separates the bowels from the lungs), the cause of which was the rupture of a small vessel that attached the gut with the body, and the right kidney was congested.

When asked about the cause of these unusual injuries, Dr. Gyorfi said, "I think it was caused by some external violence unknown to me. But I don't think it was caused by the rope." He continued to say, "I would think the deceased fell down and hit with her body some relatively large and relatively hard surface. I think this because the injury was so symmetrical. Also at the same time I found injuries to both shoulders."

With the autopsy result in hand, on Sunday February 3 at 1:30 P.M., Corporal Duff and Sergeant Finney went to the County jail to get Mr.

Morrison. They returned to Dan's home to question him in light of this new information. When they arrived at the Morrison house, he started a fire and sat down by the stove. The police looked around the premises for two hours, and Constable Brook was sent to question neighbours. Then they went into the kitchen. Dan stayed in the kitchen and kept the fire going because it was very cold that day. Mr. Morrison was sitting at the end of the stove while the Mounties were searching the premises. Then Sgt. Finney sat down almost in front of the stove and put his feet in the oven to warm them. The other officers sat around the kitchen. Then Sgt. Finney said: "The autopsy on your wife has been completed. There are a few points I would like to get cleared up. The autopsy shows she had some internal injuries including broken ribs, and that she died from being hanged – asphyxiation." Sgt. Finney told Mr. Morrison that he had given a statement to Cpl. Duff the previous day and if there was anything he wished to change it would be perfectly in order to do so.

Sergeant Finney was under the impression that Mrs. Morrison had either fallen or had been pushed from the front stairs of the house. With that in mind he said to Mr. Morrison "Did you push her?" That leading question might have been the opening Dan needed to launch into his story about pushing her, never mentioning that he struck her with a skillet.

Dan said, "Well, you fellows have treated me pretty fairly, I will tell you the whole story. Yes. I pushed her."

Sgt. Finney asked, "Why did you push her?"

Dan said, "I was having my breakfast – and as a consequence of an argument with my wife the previous night, she was screaming at me, and finally made a remark. She was standing on the kitchen floor near the couch. She called me a 'whore's bastard.'"

Then Sergeant Finney, who had accompanied Corporal Duff to this second interview with Dan Morrison, asked Dan to show how he hanged his wife. Without hesitation, Dan demonstrated with a piece of rope how he had tied the knot and placed the noose around the neck of his wife. Cpl. Duff played the part of victim Daisy, while Sgt. Finney and Cst. Tiller watched. Dan threw the rope over the banister, drew it up a certain distance, and then tied the knot.

Corporal Duff and Sergeant Finney decided it was time to take a second statement (C/2) from Dan Morrison. The statement follows:

Baddeck Forks, N.S.

STATEMENT of Daniel Murdock Morrison of Baddeck Forks, Feb. 3rd, 1957
Victoria County, N.S.

Further to the statement given by me to Corporal Duff of the R.C.M.Police on the 2nd day of February 1957 at which time I was warned as follows and understand same- "You need not say anything you have nothing to hope from any promise or favour and nothing to fear from any threat whether or not you say anything, anything you do say may be used as evidence." Since I gave that statement I have had considerable conversation with the police and I understand that the warning given me by Corporal DUFF yesterday and previously referred to still holds good with regard to anything that I may have said to the police and anything I am about to say regarding the death of my wife Daisy (Mrs. Daniel Murdock) MORRISON.

The Police referred to are Sgt. FINNEY. Cpl. DUFF, Constable TILLER and Constable BROOK all of the R.C.M.P. that have been investigating the death of my wife.

At no time have any of these Police officers mistreated me, threatened me, promised me anything or held out any inducements to me, and anything I have said or about to give in this statement is voluntary and of my own free will.

During the past four years at least my wife and I have not been getting along at all. During the last two winters I have not been home as I was working away and only came home on week-ends now and again. This winter I have been home steady since before Christmas and my wife and I have had considerable trouble with the arguments getting stronger as time went on. She was always after me about various things and made life miserable in general. She had gone so far as she would get me sent to the Asylum if it was the last thing she would do on this earth.

I met my wife through a lonely hearts club in 1949 or 1950 and we were married in July or August of 1950. I married her because I wanted companionship and a house keeper. However she was never a wife to me. During the period we were married life was far from pleasant and at times was hell on earth. During the last three or four weeks due to my wife's nagging I could not sleep and stayed awake half the night, often times hearing 2 or 3 o'clock striking and during the day could not do my work in the woods and hated to come home for dinner or my meals. Finally on Saturday February 2nd, 1957 after her nagging me during the night of February 1st and keeping me awake with her screaming, shouting, cursing and swearing from the time I went to bed at 11.00 P.M. until 1.00 o'clock when she went to bed, the argument was so bad first thing in the morning just after she got up and before she had breakfast, that day about 8.00 A.M. the 2-2-57 while she was standing on the kitchen floor near the couch she called me a " Whore's Bastard", that I pushed her and she lost her balance and fell against the corner of the couch striking her chest on the corner of the couch, and knocking herself out. I picked her up and carried her from the kitchen into the front hall where it was cooler and sat her on a kitchen chair which was there. After I had placed her on the chair she fell off sideways and fell on the floor striking the left side of her head on a telephone insulator that was on the floor. This cut her head and caused a lot of bleeding. I left her laying on the floor in the hallway on her back with her head in a pool of blood. When I saw her laying on the floor suffering I lost my presence of mind and went upstairs to where I knew there was a rope and I cut a piece off with my pocket knife. The rope was in a back room we used as a toilet. I brought the rope down and tied a loop in the end of it and then ran the rope through the loop forming a slip noose- she was still unconscious- and I placed the noose around her neck and pulled it tight on the lower part of her neck. I held onto the rope and went up the stairs holding it tight and standing on the stairs I threw the end of the rope over the top railing and pulled the rope raising my wife until she was clear of the floor and hanging suspended by the rope around her neck. I then tied the rope to the top rail after winding the rope a couple of times and made it fast. While I was pulling my wife up her foot caught the chair and upset it and I think her shoe came off at this time. She did not struggle or make any noise.

I then came down stairs and got a wet mop that was behind the stove and mopped the blood off the hall floor, because I couldn't bear to see the blood on the floor. I then washed the mop out in a pale [sic] of water and wrung it out with my hands, placed the mop behind the stove and threw the water out in the yard and dried my hands on a towel at the sink.

The blood on the rope by which my wife was hanging got on the rope while I was placing the rope around her neck and coming in contact with the blood on the floor and her hair.

At this time I was dressed to go to the woods. I had my breakfast and my wife didn't. I then put my cap on and went to the woods to work. This was around 8:30 A.M. of the 2nd of February 1957. I worked in the woods for the remainder of the morning and I returned to the house around 1:15 P.M. I was working about a quarter of a mile from the house piling pulp and cleaning brush off the road. When I left the house I locked the back door and the other had been nailed up for the winter. When I returned I unlocked the back door, entered the house and saw my wife still hanging where I had left her. I did not touch her but went to the phone and called Alex MacLean to have him come over right away. I did not tell him what I wanted as he didn't ask.

I then went outside and waited untul Alex MacLean came a short time later. When he arrived he asked if there was something wrong and I said yes. I believe I said my wife had hung herself. We both went in the house where I showed him where my wife was hanging. MacLean told me I had better call the doctor and I did. I called his office and a woman answered and I asked her to send the doctor as it was an emergency. She asked what it was so I told her my wife was hanging in the hall, and she said she would try and get the doctor. He came on the phone and asked me to meet him at the road as he would be right out.

Alex MacLean left and went to get Mr. and Mrs. Dan

Neil MacMillan who are also neighbours and I went down to the road to meet the doctor. I did not lock the door when I went down to the road. Doctor C.L. MacMillan came along shortly and he examined my wife by just looking at her and he told me it was a case for the R.C.M.P. and he went to the phone and called the police in Baddeck. Shortly after Doctor MacMillan arrived, Alex MacLean, Dan Neil MacMillan and his wife arrived. After remaining a short time doctor MacMillan went down to the road and Alex MacLean went to meet the police and Dan Neil MacMillan and his wife remained with me until the Police and Coroner arrived.

My wife had not been moved from where I had hanged her until she was removed by the police and the undertaker later that evening. The piece of rope shown me by the Police is the rope from which I cut off a piece of rope to hang my wife with. This statement is correct and as far as I'm concerned it is the same as if it were given under oath. I'm willing to swear to the contents of this statement.

Signed witnesses: Signed:
A.L. Duff Cpl.   Dan M. Morrison
F.H. Finney Sgt.

After the statement was signed, Dan was arrested and taken to the Victoria County jail to await trial. Dan Murdock Morrison's trial began on May 28, 1957, and lasted through June 1, 1957.

He was found guilty of the hanging murder of his wife, Daisy. He was sentenced to be hanged on the 21st day of August 1957. Following an appeal, his sentence was changed to manslaughter on Friday, October 4th 1957, and he was sentenced to fourteen years in Dorchester Penitentiary in New Brunswick[37].

---

37 Trial transcripts are in Appendix C.

Chapter Nine

The Rest of the Story

Author's *Note*: An excellent seven-part series about the murder, trial and Dan Morrison's life after prison was published by the *Cape Breton Highlander* newspaper in 1981. This newspaper is no longer published. Following here, with permission, are sections of the series. These sections cover the arrest, trial, sentencing and Dan's life after prison.

> HIGHLANDER, Sept. 2, 1981 Part IV
> Daisy laid to rest
> Dan Murdoch Changes Story: arrested for wife's murder

"The story Dan Morrison told the Mounties who escorted him back to his Baddeck Forks home, was very different from the one he had told them the day before.

Daisy's body had been removed from where it had been found hanging from the stair rail in the hallway. Sgt. F.H. Finney and Cpl. A.L. Duff sat in the now cozy farm kitchen and sipped tea Dan Murdoch had prepared after they got the fire going and the house warmed up.

As he sat in a rocker by the kitchen range speaking quietly, Dan Murdoch had his guests' undivided attention. Corporal Duff took notes and transcribed them later into a formal statement. Dan Murdock even demonstrated using Duff as a 'victim', how he accomplished the grisly feat. We quote his revised statement verbatim[38].

On the strength of the February 3, 1957 statement and the results of the autopsy, Daniel Murdoch 'Spinney' Morrison was removed to Baddeck that same night and charged with the murder of his wife, Daisy Delinger-Leadley-Fisher-Morrison, who at that moment was being prepared for burial[39].

Dan spent the night in a jail cell in Baddeck – this time with the door securely locked – and Daisy's last mortal remains were placed in a 'boat', a bottom of the

---

38   Author's Note: His first (C/1) and later revised statement (C/2) are shown in Chapter 8.
39   Author's Note: It was not known at the time that Daisy's birth surname was McEachen. She had left that surname long in the past for reasons that will become clear later.

line casket, the roughest and cheapest available. She was waked in the tiny church at Big Baddeck with only a half dozen people in attendance for the final service. The casket had to be strapped to a horse-drawn sled to get it through the heavy drifts to the little cemetery. There Daisy was committed to the cold, cold ground. The only sounds breaking the incredible stillness were the scrape of shovel on frozen earth and the snorting of the impatient horse[40].

HIGHLANDER, Sept. 9, 1981
For wife's murder - 1957
Dan Murdoch Morrison "brought to justice[41]"

"Dan Murdoch 'Spinney' Morrison was formally charged with the murder of his wife Daisy at 11p.m. on Saturday, February 3, 1957, a day after she was found hanging from a seven-foot length of rope in their Baddeck Forks farmhouse. Commissioner Charles McCurdy presided at Baddeck Court House.

Dan Murdoch reappeared the following morning at 10 a.m., this time before Magistrate John F. MacDonald, for a formal hearing into the charge. Dr. C.L. MacMillan recommended at this hearing that Dan Murdoch be sent to the Nova Scotia Hospital for psychiatric examination. His recommendation was followed and the hearing was adjourned indefinitely to await the psychiatrist's report. Ironically one of the doctors involved in the examination was Dr. Fraser Nicholson whose parents had lived in Baddeck, and who himself was a fairly regular visitor to the Village. Dr. Nicholson was not personally acquainted with Dan Murdoch, however.

After a 30-day stay at the Nova Scotia Hospital, Dan Murdoch was pronounced mentally competent to answer the charge of murder. The decision of the psychiatrists was received on March 9th and the machinery of justice

---

40   Author's Note: The grave site remains unmarked; the notation on the old plot map shows her as D. Morrison.
41   Highlander, September 9, 1981

was oiled up and put in motion to handle the first murder case heard in Victoria County in 21 years.

R. Fisher Hudson, now MLA and Minister of Housing in the Buchanan government, was Crown prosecutor at the time. He was assisted in preparing the crown's case by Harris MacDonald of the Attorney General's department. Appearing in Dan Murdoch's defence was the late Donald C. MacNeil then an MLA in the Stanfield government and his father John MacNeil QC, his law partner[42].

Magistrate John F. MacDonald again presided at the preliminary hearing held on March 18, and five witnesses were called to give evidence. They included Alex MacLean, Dan Murdoch's neighbour; Sgt. F.H. Finney and Cpl. A.L. Duff; the RCMP officers who headed the investigation; Dr. C.L. MacMillan, who first examined the body and Dr. A.W. Gyorfi who performed the autopsy.

Besides the evidence of the five witnesses called to the stand, Dan Murdoch's two statements were read into the court record despite the strenuous objections of defence counsel Donald MacNeil. It was decided that there was sufficient evidence to bind the accused over for trial, and Dan Murdoch was ordered to appear at the May sitting of the Nova Scotia Supreme Court before Mr. Justice L.D. Currie.

Forty-eight people were called for jury duty – Dan Murdoch himself among them. It is perhaps not surprising in an area with a relatively sparse population that the accused's name should be picked. But there was no legal precedent to cover the situation and his name was allowed to stand. He was, of course, excused from duty as were 16 others who asked for exemptions on various grounds – mainly relationship to the accused. After considerable and jockeying and objections to candidates by both defence and prosecution, a panel of a dozen peers was finally selected to decide on the

---

42   J. Smith MacIvor Q.C. who mortgaged the property to Dan Morrison in 1945 was defeated in the October 1956 election by Donald MacNeil. Mr. MacNeil was MLA at the time of the trial.

innocence or guilt of Dan Murdoch Morrison. Leonard Harvey was selected as foreman.

Dan Morrison, in the meantime, ignored the storm clouds gathering round his head and the legal wrangling and hubbub at the centre of which he stood. Since his return from the Nova Scotia Hospital he spent his days quietly in his cell, praying most of the time and showing little interest in his own defence. His only voiced regret was that it was necessary to keep an around the clock guard on him. He didn't want to be a nuisance to his captors, he said but if the law demanded it there was nothing he could do. His only worry was his tool box at home, which he asked his jailers to keep safe. Dan Murdoch seemed more concerned with how he would fare in the next world than in this one.

It was this state of mind that allowed him to enter the court room with total composure when his trial began on Tuesday, May 28, 1957."

Highlander News continues...

HIGHLANDER, Sept. 16, 1981
For 1957 slaying of wife Daisy
Dan Murdoch goes on trial; jury reaches verdict quickly

Between the time he was arrested for his wife's murder on February 3rd, 1957 and his appearance at the spring session of the Nova Scotia Supreme Court on May 28th, Dan Murdoch Morrison of Baddeck Forks "put his house in order". He spent most of his waking hours in the Baddeck jail on his knees, deep in prayer.

When he appeared for trial before Justice L.D. Currie he was totally composed and seldom took his eyes off the witness stand. He listened intently to the witnesses as they took the stand, mainly the same people who had testified at the preliminary hearing. There were the Mounties who had done the investigating, Dr. C.L. MacMillan who had examined the body and Alex

MacLean the neighbour Dan Murdoch had summoned to his house on the day of the murder. Another witness was Dr. A.W. Gyorfi, the pathologist who had performed the autopsy on Daisy's remains.

Dr. Gyorfi's testimony was long and detailed. He told of finding that the victim had suffered 14 fractured ribs, a fractured throat bone, bruises on the shoulders, a cut on the temple and ruptured blood vessels in the stomach. He also found two marks on the victim's throat. One mark was a deep furrow above the Adam's apple, while the second was about a half inch below and less pronounced. He expressed the opinion that the two marks could have been caused by the rope slipping immediately after application. The injuries were all inflicted before death and, in essence, he said they were consistent with Dan Murdoch's account of how Daisy met her death.

A great deal of time was spent wrangling over the admissibility of Dan Murdoch's statement to police. The jury was dismissed while "a trial within a trial" was conducted into the matter, but in the end Justice Currie ruled that they should be read into the court record, overruling the argument put forth by defence counsel Donald C. MacNeil. MacNeil claimed the RCMP used psychological fear to get the statements. He said there was pressure used which resulted in intimidation. He said the accused should have been questioned at headquarters instead of in his own house, and that giving him a "night's lodging" in the jail before he was charged was also intimidating. He argued that by drinking tea with the accused the Mounties had put him in a mental state that was never removed by the statutory police warning. But Justice Currie didn't buy the arguments, and Sgt. Finney took the stand to recount Dan Murdoch's story.

This was the only time during the proceedings when the accused lost his composure. He slumped forward in his chair in the prisoner's box and refused to look at the Mountie, resuming his normal demeanour only after Finney had left the stand.

The trial went on for three full days and was well into the fourth day before the jury retired to consider the evidence and bring in their verdict. In his charge to the jury Mr. Justice Currie told them only two verdicts were possible - guilty of murder, or not guilty. He ruled out manslaughter on the grounds of provocation.

"It is my decision as a matter of law which you are bound to take from me, that there is not any, not the slightest evidence of a wrongful act which would entitle the jury to consider the defence of provocation. Therefore I withdraw from the jury the issue of manslaughter on the grounds of provocation."

Mr. Justice Currie said he was satisfied that the accused was "not propelled by the operation of passion" when he hanged his wife. He pointed out that the accused did not kill his wife by pushing her. "After she fell against the couch he had sufficient presence of mind to know his wife was not dead. I am satisfied that while he was downstairs he took the time to plan and think what he intended to do with the rope."

In his 90-minute charge to the jury he made it clear what he felt the verdict should be. "The woman, Mrs. Morrison, was a human being, not a dog or cat that broke a leg and should be shot."

Crown Prosecutor Fisher Hudson addressed the jury for 45 minutes, calling the events in the Morrison home on Feb. 2 "murder, cruel and calculated."

Defence counsel Donald MacNeil spoke for 50 minutes, stressing the situation in the Morrison home, citing the effect of a nagging wife who threatened her husband with commitment to an asylum.

When the jury finally retired on the fourth day of the trial, they took only 75 minutes to reach their decision. At 3:50 p.m. on Friday, May 31, 1957, foreman Leonard Harvey announced the jury's verdict. Dan Murdoch hardly flinched when he heard the "guilty" verdict read. He thanked his defence counsel as he left the prisoner's dock and walked past the jury to his cell. His private reaction is illustrated in his statement when he reached his cell, "When you're at peace with God, you have nothing to fear."

Mr. Justice Currie lauded the jury for the verdict saying he agreed completely with it and the RCMP for their "high type of investigation." He had words of praise also for Mr. Hudson and Mr. MacDonald for the prosecution, and for Donald MacNeil for his "energetic defence."

While the jury had entered a plea for mercy, it could have no effect on the sentence. First degree murder carried a mandatory death sentence and on July 3, 1957, Mr. Justice Currie intoned the words: "The sentence of the court is that you be taken from this place to a lawful prison and there be detained until August 21, 1957, and then be taken to a place of execution, and then you shall be hanged by the neck until you are dead. And may God have mercy on your soul."

Dan Murdoch was reported as stoic as he had been throughout the four day trial receiving his sentence with bowed head, then summoning a guard to take him back to his cell.

Donald MacNeil wasted no time in announcing that he would launch an appeal on the grounds that the judge had misdirected the jury by ruling out manslaughter through provocation. Dan Murdoch's fate wasn't sealed yet. (Continued next week)

HIGHLANDER, Sept. 23, 1957
"Learned Trial Judge erred";
Dan Murdock gets new trial

After the June 1st death sentence was handed down, Dan Murdoch Morrison's legal counsel wasted no time in launching an appeal. The document drawn up by defender Donald C. MacNeil, MLA, and signed by Dan Murdoch himself was dispatched to the Supreme Court of Nova Scotia on June 7th, 1957.

MacNeil was not kind to Justice L.D. Currie in stating his grounds for appealing his client's conviction on the charge of murdering his wife Daisy. Defence counsel claimed the "Learned Trial Judge erred" on no less than seven points in his handling of the case, particularly in his charge to the jury. An excerpt from the appeal application follows:

"(1) The Learned Trial Judge erred in that he failed to give proper consideration to the circumstances which reflected on the voluntary nature of an incriminating statement taken from the accused by officers of the RCMP on the third day of February, A.D. 1957.

"(2) The Learned Trial Judge erred in that he admitted the involuntary statement (C2) in evidence at the trial.

"(3) The Learned Trial Judge erred in that he decided questions of fact which he ought to have left for the jury.

"(4) The Learned Trial Judge erred in that he did not state fairly to the jury the case for the accused, particularly with regard to evidence concerning the amount of weight to be attached to the statements referred to in paragraphs (1) and (2) of this application.

"(5) The Learned Trial Judge erred in that having explained the law of provocation to the jury he did not permit the jury to decide from the facts whether or not provocation applied.

"(6) The Learned Trial Judge erred in that he instructed the jury that they had only two possible verdicts 'Guilty' or 'Not Guilty'.

"(7) The charge of the Learned Trial Judge was unfair, inflammatory and prejudiced to the accused."

The eighth point left room for further criticism of the Judge's interpretation of the law: "(8) And such other grounds as may appear when I or my Counsel have a transcript of the evidence at the trial."

On June 21st word was received that a hearing would be held into the application for appeal before the full bench of the Nova Scotia Supreme Court on July 10, 1957 in Halifax. As prosecution and defence prepared their submissions for the hearing and neighbours in Baddeck scurried about with a petition urging commutation of his death sentence, Dan Murdoch showed little interest in the proceedings. Just 42 days away from the gallows he remained as stoical as he had been throughout the trial. Under 24-hour guard in the Baddeck jail, the prisoner spent most of his time in prayer, "making his peace with God."

Defence counsel argued his case for more than three hours, and the prosecution took two hours to present the Crown's side. Donald C. MacNeil stressed misdirection of the jury when the Judge ruled out manslaughter and admittance to evidence of statements which in effect were confessions. He claimed the statements were not given voluntarily, and cited what he called "fraternization" between the Mounties and the accused before the statements were obtained. The Judge should have allowed the jury to decide whether or not provocation applied, MacNeil argued.

On the prosecution side, Crown solicitor Fisher Hudson and Harris MacDonald of the Attorney General's department presented the Crown's case in opposition to the appeal application. They vigorously defended Currie's handling of the trial, claiming that "... it is submitted the charge to the jury will be found fair to the accused in every way."

After a full day of hearing evidence, the Court reserved decision on the application. If the Bench rejected the appeal requested, the accused would be hanged on August 21. Even one dissenting vote would allow the defence to carry the case to the Supreme Court of Canada. On July 28 the announcement came. Dan Murdock was granted a retrial, and as no request had been made for a special sitting of the court, he was slated to appear at the regular session in October.

On Tuesday, October 1, the retrial got under way before Mr. Justice Eugene Parker. It was pretty much a repeat of the first trial, with the same defence and prosecution lawyers, and the same witnesses giving the same testimony. Defence again argued bitterly against admission of Dan Murdock's statements, and again was overruled by the trial judge. The proceedings began on Tuesday and continued through Wednesday and Thursday, with a night session on Thursday.

The participants addressed the jury Friday morning and the panel retired in the afternoon to consider the evidence. Judge Parker advised the jury it could bring in one of three verdicts: murder, manslaughter or acquittal. After 40 minutes of deliberation foreman Alex Wilkie of Sugar Loaf read the jury's verdict: Dan Murdock Morrison was found guilty on a reduced charge of manslaughter.

Dan Murdock was reported visibly relieved at the verdict. After Judge Parker handed down a sentence of fourteen years in Dorchester Penitentiary, the accused shook hands with his lawyer and returned to his cell to await transfer to the penitentiary.

HIGHLANDER, Continues
Sept 30, 1981
Dan Murdock out on parole picks up pieces

Dan Murdock Morrison, having been sentenced to fourteen years imprisonment for the rope slaying of his wife, Daisy, was quietly transferred from Baddeck jail to Dorchester Penitentiary. He had been in the Baddeck lockup since his arrest in February. The lengthy trial and subsequent appeal had been almost nine months, and Dan Murdock had spent the entire time behind bars, except for his 30 days in the Nova Scotia Hospital for psychiatric examination.

When long time employer J. (Bill) Stephens went to see him at Baddeck, Dan Murdock was glad Bill's father wasn't around to see the terrible turn of events. Mr. Stephens, on the other hand, was completely taken by surprise when he heard of Dan Murdock's troubles. He apparently shared the opinion of most people who knew him that the accused was a mild-mannered, soft spoken type, unlikely to get into the predicament he found himself in. Others admitted Dan Murdock had a short fuse, given to outbursts of rage when crossed. This side of his nature, coupled with the toothbrush moustache he affected at one time, earned him the nickname "Hitler."

Whatever the people believed, the law had dealt with Dan Murdock in its own fashion, and he was on his way to Dorchester, New Brunswick in October, 1957 to begin serving the sentence Justice Eugene Parker had handed down.

Little is known of his time in the penitentiary. He had no visitors and obviously caused no trouble, because after only four years Dan Murdock Morrison was granted parole from the National Parole Board in Ottawa. The terms of his release were that he "proceed directly to Sydney, Nova Scotia," report to the Police Chief of that city and not leave the area without his permission. The John Howard Society helped cushion his re-entry into society, and in October, 1961, Dan Murdock found himself settled into a boarding house on Charlotte Street, ready to face the future or not.

The task ahead of him was awesome. Almost 70, Dan Murdock had to start from scratch and build some sort of life for himself. The task was made almost insurmountable by the fact that he was virtually penniless...*Daisy's estate had been administered by the old Nova Scotia Trust Company, who simply ordered the tenants who were buying her house on Fisher Street by instalment, to pay off the debt in total. This they did, turning over the $700 they owed to the Trust Company. This went into a fund that was fattened by a little over $300 in a bank account in Baddeck and a similar sum in a Sydney bank. Thus Daisy's estate, officially at least, totalled only $1400...*

Her estate was cleared up very quickly by the administrators, and after the period prescribed by law, Daisy's estate was claimed by the County of Victoria there being no heirs.

However, the fact remains that he had to pick up the tatters of his life without a penny to his name. Perhaps the most heartbreaking fact was that even his tool box, the one possession he asked should be kept safe, was gone along with everything else.

He applied almost immediately for the old age pension, and ran into trouble because his birth was registered many years after the event, and he had difficulty establishing his eligibility. He looked for work, but without the tools of his trade and at his advanced age, he found there was none available to him. Whatever years were left to him looked pretty bleak for Dan Murdock.

Author's Note: I ask the reader to keep in mind my italicized section of the *Highlander* story that mentions Daisy's estate value being $1400 plus. Then study the August and September 1957 mortgage and sale documents Nos. 17603, 17770, 17777, and 17778. Notice the $1500 sale price in Document 17,770 Recital 2. Contrast this with the $800 mortgage in the 20 December 1945 document 17,603. These recorded documents may be found at the Victoria County Registry of Deeds, Baddeck, NS. Ask yourself 'what became of Daisy's $1400-$1500 bank account after her death?' Her murderer spouse could not inherit it by law. Victoria County did not confiscate it. Had she lived and paid off the amount due with her last dollar, she would have owned the house and property. If she died of natural cause after that, Dan Murdock 'Spinney' Morrison, her then husband, would have inherited it. Daisy, however, died penniless, like her father and mother in 1894.

Later you will learn that Dan's original attorney, J. Smith MacIvor, lost the 1956 election to Barrister MacNeil, and reactivated his neglected practice in November or December. Could he have notified Dan and Daisy that the ten-year unpaid mortgage needed to be paid or foreclosure initiated? Could this be the reason that 73-year-old Daisy was extremely agitated and hysterical? Could it be that Dan asked her for her last dollars so they would not be evicted in winter with no money and no place to live? Could it also be that, after her murder, her estate was used to pay the overdue mortgage of $1500? Could this be the incendiary reason why Daisy was so very, very upset on the evening and morning of February 1 and 2? I leave the mystery for you, dear reader, to solve. The clue might be in the legal documents surrounding ownership of the house at Baddeck Forks. You decide!

> NO. 17603
> MORTGAGE
> Page 140
>
> Registered at 9.45 a.m. of the 18th day of February, A.D., 1957 on the oath of Rob. MacLellan
>
> Registrar of Deeds
>
> THIS INDENTURE made this twentieth day of December in the year of Our Lord One Thousand Nine Hundred and forty-five.
>
> BETWEEN: DANIEL MURDOCK MORRISON, of Forkes Baddeck, in the County of Victoria, Province of Nova Scotia, hereinafter called the MORTGAGOR
>
> of the One Part, and
>
> JOHN SMITH MACIVOR, Barrister, of Sydney, in the County of Cape Breton, Province of Nova Scotia, Executor of the Estate of Roderick A. MacLeod, late of Forkes Baddeck, in the County of Victoria, Province of Nova Scotia, hereinafter called the MORTGAGEE
>
> of the Other Part
>
> WITNESSETH That the said Mortgagor for and in consideration of the sum of Eight Hundred ($800.00) Dollars of lawful money of the Dominion of Canada, to the said Mortgagee in hand well and truly paid by the said Mortgagor at or before the ensealing and delivery of These PRESENTS, (the receipt whereof is hereby acknowledged) bargained, sold, aliened, eneoffed, released, remised, conveyed and confirmed, and by These Presents doth grant, bargain, sell, alien, eneoff, release, remise, convey, and confirm unto the said Mortgagee

Document No. 17603 (partial)

$800.00 plus 5% interest Mortgage indenture made 20 December 1945 for purchase of MacLeod property at Baddeck Forks

BETWEEN:
DANIEL MURDOCK MORRISON, MORTGAGOR
and
JOHN SMITH MACIVOR, MORTGAGEE
Registered 18th February 1957
Released 13th August 1957

HIGHLANDER, October 14, 1981
The good old, bad old, last days
Fate plays its last cruel trick on Dan Murdock

Dan Murdock Morrison of Baddeck Forks was released from Dorchester Penitentiary having served four years of a 14-year sentence for the murder of his wife

Daisy. Designated parolee number 5725, he was granted his release on October 18, 1961, but was ordered to live within the terms of his parole agreement until April 7, 1968. His re-entry into society wasn't smooth. He was penniless, had no home, and being over 70 by this time, he couldn't find work in his carpentry trade. The future didn't look promising to say the least.

It was a fateful day when he got word that an old friend and distant cousin was very sick and had left her home in North River to stay with her daughter in Sydney. Dan Murdock got his courage up to visit. It was a turning point, for it brought him in contact with Ella MacLeod and her husband Billy. Ella had been adopted into the home of Christie Effie MacDonald of North River Bridge, and had known Dan Murdock since childhood. Curiously she had a soft spot for the old man and made him welcome in her home. Eventually, Dan Murdock went to live with the MacLeods[43].

Ella's husband worked at the steel plant and the family's fortunes closely followed the ups and downs of the plant during the uncertain sixties. During the periodic layoffs, the MacLeods would head for North River and Dan Murdock went with them. This brought him into conflict with the terms of his parole and brought a nervous letter from Police Chief Vincent Campbell to whom he was supposed to report once a month.

Campbell wanted to know why he hadn't heard from Dan Murdock for almost sixty days, but left him lots of room to manoeuvre, suggesting perhaps he was sick or found it difficult to get transportation, and asking that he phone or write so that the routine parole form could be sent off. The letter brought a visit from Billy MacLeod who assured the Police Chief he had no cause to worry, and subsequently Dan Murdock's parole was amended so he had to check in only every three months.

Campbell was also instrumental in getting Dan Murdock a shift guarding a fire alarm box on Halloween,

---

43   Mrs. MacLeod very kindly provided photographs of the Morrison family. A complete genealogy of Dan Murdock's family is being gathered by Shawna Morrison in Alberta.

though then MP Malcolm "Vic" MacInnis got the credit. As a result Dan Murdock changed his allegiance at the polls for only the second time in his life, voting NDP in support of MacInnis. The only other time he had forsaken his favoured Liberal Party was to vote for his friend Dan K. MacLeod, a Tory who was running for Councillor against Gordon Harvey. Dan Murdock's switch wasn't enough; Harvey won by a single vote.

Dan Murdock seemed to enjoy life in North River. At first he was reclusive, afraid to venture out for fear of running into bad feelings from the neighbours. It was for this reason he never went back to Baddeck after he was released from prison. Eventually, though he was persuaded to go to church when the minister from Baddeck, Rev. Nelson MacDonald was guest preacher at North River. Rev. MacDonald gave him a warm welcome, as did the rest of the congregation, and Dan Murdock never looked back.

He finally got his pension – all of $55 a month, and promptly turned $35 a month of it over to Mrs. MacLeod to pay for his keep. He even tried to build kitchen cupboards for her, but he hadn't the proper tools and being over 70 didn't have the physical stamina to accomplish such a big job. Ominously his mental faculties were beginning to deteriorate also.

By the Fall of 1968 Dan Murdock was in such bad shape that Mrs. MacLeod put him in hospital, hoping he could be rehabilitated sufficiently to allow her to continue to look after him at home. But he had lost control of both physical and mental faculties, and was sent to Nova Scotia Hospital again for a period of observation.

The diagnosis was simple but irreversible senility brought about by hardening of the arteries. Dr. Fraser Nicholson had reported the onset of the condition when he examined Dan Murdock before the trial 11 years earlier.

So, the string had run out for Dan Murdock. And in a last cruel trick of fate, he was sent from the Nova Scotia Hospital to live out his days at the Cape Breton County

Hospital. This made him the second of Daisy's husbands to die in that institution, and fulfilled Daisy's promise to have him committed to an asylum[44].

Mrs. Macleod visited him there and found him quite content in his last days; perhaps the irony of the situation escaped him in his befuddled state.

Dan Murdock Morrison died on May 25, 1969 at the Cape Breton County Hospital. Perhaps it's understandable that a man who brought so much notoriety and shame upon an otherwise highly respected family should be given a swift send-off. But the scene at Fillmore's Funeral Home was grim as only three mourners showed up besides his sister and her family. There were no death notices published, and by the time most people heard of his demise Dan Murdock had already been committed to the cold ground at Hardwood Hill Cemetery.

Dan Murdock outlived his parole by more than a year, and officially he died a free man. But his grave remains unmarked to this day.

So who had the last word? Dan Murdock, who had his way and silenced the nagger forever? Or Daisy, who perhaps was cackling over Dan Murdock ending his days in an asylum?

At this distance, and from the outside, it would seem that the only winners were those who divided the worldly goods Dan Murdock and Daisy were so jealous of. He wouldn't leave because he owned the house. She wouldn't leave because she had spent money on the house. In the end they both left; and not of their own choosing.

Hopefully the principals in this awful drama are finally resting in peace.

End of the Highlander Newspaper Series.

---

44   The Cape Breton Hospital was known by locals as the insane asylum. But it was much more a hospital for seniors with senility and patients with severe medical conditions.

Epilogue

Big Glen Today

Today, Big Glen is practically empty of people. Only three small families live along Daisy Delinger McEachen Leadley Fisher Morrison and Dan Murdock 'Spinney' Morrison's dirt road at Baddeck Forks. When these old people pass on, unless some new families move in, the Glen will be dead. In reality, it is dead already. Daisy's spirit hovers over...watching and waiting.

Now it is past time for fables, rumours and jokes to end. Dan Murdock 'Spinney' Morrison and Daisy McEachen Leadley Fisher Morrison were basically good people. As Shawna Morrison says: "I wish Dan and Daisy were here to be able to show us what kind of people they really were. But I know that one day, when it's all our turns to be present with God, as soon as we ask about it, He definitely will show us the undeniable truth from both sides of the story. Like Jesus said, we are all held accountable for all we do.... the best sake for all is to look at all people in a more compassionate way. This way nobody gets ridiculed any longer – not Daisy and not Dan."

Nobody is perfect. People come together to get their basic needs met. But it is most important to communicate and be honourable and fair in marriage and relationships. Daisy had needs stretching back to her childhood. Needs suppressed by fear and loss. Mother and father abandoned their very young children in a harsh, jungle-like environment. She needed the attention of a loving, caring father. She carried the fears of her mother—fears about poverty, a depressed husband, no money coming in to support the family and the new child in her womb.

Daisy probably held the resentment of her father's leaving the family destitute, and therefore money was the salvation she needed to survive. She needed reassurance, love, peace of mind and heart. She and Dan both needed each other in different ways, but never properly communicated it to each other to plan it together. They were elderly – she 66 and he 59 – when they married. She was 73 and he 66 when he killed her. They never married for love. They married to fill specific needs: she had a need to be needed and loved; he for companionship and housekeeping. Her pride was in being an excellent housekeeper, cleaning every nook and cranny and demanding of herself to have everything orderly in her environment. But she also needed companionship and gratitude, and a man to replace her father who rejected her in 1894.

Daisy proved to be a loyal, trustworthy and hard-working domestic servant, as her ten-year tenure with the Lownds' shows us. Her twenty-year marriage to Frederick William Leadley, her ten-year marriage to Albert Fisher, and her seven-year marriage to Dan Morrison—this one lived amidst tension, frustration, depression and ill health—show that Daisy followed her mother's last words, "Be good." Daisy was a very good friend and caretaker to the men and women who needed her services. Unfortunately, Dan Murdock 'Spinney' Morrison was not a man who needed much of anything from a woman. He escaped into the woods or stayed away for days, sometimes weeks, when Daisy wanted to discuss finances or social issues or simply relax with her husband. No wonder she became frustrated, angry and fearful!

Too late, Daisy learned that Dan had no deed to the house she had restored to a proper home, nor to the property on which she lived. Was her husband living a lie? Was there some valid reason for the missing recorded deed?

Is it possible J. Smith MacIvor, because of illness or his busyness in running for and occupying public office, (from 1942-1956) could not follow up to collect the unpaid mortgage loan? Did he put too much trust in Dan to do the proper thing: pay the loan and record the Deed? Perhaps Dan believed that his lawyer had handled all the sale details and there was nothing more to do? But why was the property still recorded in MacIvor's name on Victoria County registry from sale date until August, 1957? The mortgage-loan legal documents were in perfect legal order.

Is it possible that Mr. MacIvor felt a deep sense of failure when Dan was sentenced to death by hanging? He died ten days later, perhaps stressed of knowing that if Dan had not or could not pay, as appears to be the case, he should have been confronted, legally, long before 1957. Then Daisy might never have met Dan or moved to Baddeck Forks and died there. She could have lived in her home on Fisher Street and died of natural causes, surrounded by her friends in Sydney. This, of course, is speculation on my part.

I am not trying to shift the blame for Daisy's murder; however, I imagine her saying to her mother at the moment she died at the end of the bloody rope, "Mother, I tried to be good like you told me." I wonder, did Alice reach for her daughter, hold her in her arms, and comfort her, saying, "I know, dear Daisy, I know. You don't have to try any more. You did a fine job of it. Now rest peacefully."

Dan Murdock 'Spinney' Morrison said it all when he was asked during his confinement and trial why he was so peaceful. His reply was "If you are right with God there's nothing to fear." Dan believed that he received forgiveness from God. Rest in Peace Dan and Daisy. You are forgiven.

St. Andrews Church is where Daisy was waked, following her hanging.

St. Andrews Church and Cemetery in Baddeck Forks, Nova Scotia

The patch of bare earth is the humble location of Daisy's unmarked grave.
The two monuments behind her are for unrelated deceased.
May she rest in peace.

Appendices

Appendix A – Dan Morrison's Genealogy

Descendants of Donald 'Spinney' Morrison

Born: 1810 in Stroud, Island of Harris, Scotland Died: in Big Baddeck, Victoria County, NS in North Gut, Victoria County, NS
m: 1843 in Big Glen, Cape Breton County, NS Died: 1926
Kate' Morrison Born: 1847 in Big Glen, Victoria County, NS Died: September 15, 1935
Born: 1841 in North River, Victoria County, NS Married: Abt 1870 Died: July 07, 1921
MacDonald Born: in North River, Victoria County, NS
…ler' MacDonald Born: in North River, Victoria County, NS
…Donald Born: in North River, Victoria County, NS
: 1851 in Big Glen, Cape Breton County, NS Died: January 04, 1946
: 1853 in Big Glen, Cape Breton County, NS
…uebec
…ex' Morrison
…d 'Archie' Morrison
…n MacArthur
…s Morrison

…son
o. Died: in Manitoba

…rrison Died: 1937 in Saskatchewan
n Born: in Kempt Head, Victoria County, NS Died: November 16, 1921 in Man O War Point, Victoria County, NS
…son
…: 1857 Died: in South Cove, Little Narrows, Victoria County, NS
m: in South Cove, Little Narrows, Victoria County, NS
Born: 1859 in Big Glen, Cape Breton County, NS Died: in Big Glen, Cape Breton County, NS
…usan
…on Died: in Big Baddeck, Victoria County, NS
…as Born: in Sydney Mines, Cape Breton County, NS Died: in Big Baddeck, Victoria County, NS
…on Died: in Boston, MA
…son Born: in Orland River, Richmond County, NS

…Morrison Born: Abt. 1896 in Big Baddeck, Victoria County, NS
…hael Born: Abt. 1895 in Moriton Pt, St Anne, Victoria County, NS Died: in Big Baddeck, Victoria County, NS
… Carmichael
…e Carmichael
…i Carmichael
…l Died: in Boston, MA
…ee Born: in Big Pond, Cape Breton County, NS
…acPhee
…rrison Born: 1862 in Big Glen, Cape Breton County, NS
Morrison Born: 1845 in Big Glen, Cape Breton County, NS Died: in Big Glen, Cape Breton County, NS
…MacLeod Born: Abt. 1854 Died: in Big Glen, Cape Breton County, NS
… Born: in Baddeck Bay, Victoria County, NS Died: in North Sydney, Cape Breton County, NS
… Kenzie Died: in North Sydney, Cape Breton County, NS
…gie' Morrison Died: in Boston, MA

f K Glen Morrison and should not be
…ing valified from other sources.

Descendants of Donald 'Spinney' Morrison

Generation No. 1

1. DONALD 'SPINNEY'³ MORRISON *(NEIL² MORRISON, BADDECK¹ MORRISON)* was born 1810 in Strond, Island of Harris, Scotland, and died in Big Baddeck, Victoria County, NS. He married CHRISTY SHAW, daughter of ALEXANDER SHAW and SARAH SHAW. She was born 1819 in North Gut, Victoria County, NS.

Notes for CHRISTY SHAW:
Resided in Big Glen, Cape Breton County, NS

Children of DONALD MORRISON and CHRISTY SHAW are:
    i. Annie⁴ Morrison, b. 1843, Big Glen, Cape Breton County, NS; d. 1926.

    Notes for Annie Morrison:
    never married

2.   ii. Catherine Morrison 'Kate' Morrison, b. 1847, Big Glen, Victoria County, NS; d. September 15, 1885.
    iii. Sarah Morrison, b. 1851, Big Glen, Cape Breton County, NS; d. January 04, 1946.

    Notes for Sarah Morrison:
    May have married Malcolm MacKenzie not MacLean. It would have been MacLean's 2nd wife.

3.   iv. Neil Morrison, b. 1853, Big Glen, Cape Breton County, NS.
    v. Mary Morrison, b. 1857; d. South Cove, Little Narrows, Victoria County, NS; m. Henry MacIver; b. South Cove, Little Narrows, Victoria County, NS.
4.   vi. Murdoch Morrison, b. 1859, Big Glen, Cape Breton County, NS; d. Big Glen, Cape Breton County, NS.
    vii. Alexandra 'Lexie' Morrison, b. 1862, Big Glen, Cape Breton County, NS.

    Notes for Alexandra 'Lexie' Morrison:
    never married

5.   viii. Alexander 'Spinney' Morrison, b. 1845, Big Glen, Cape Breton County, NS; d. Big Glen, Cape Breton County, NS.

Generation No. 2

2. CATHERINE MORRISON 'KATE'⁴ MORRISON *(DONALD 'SPINNEY'³, NEIL² MORRISON, BADDECK¹ MORRISON)* was born 1847 in Big Glen, Victoria County, NS, and died September 15, 1885. She married ANGUS MACDONALD Abt. 1870, son of DONALD MACDONALD and CATHERINE SMITH. He was born 1841 in North River, Victoria County, NS, and died July 07, 1921.

More About CATHERINE MORRISON 'KATE' MORRISON:
Burial: September 15, 1885, Goose Cove Cemetery, St. Ann's Harbour, Victoria County, NS

More About ANGUS MACDONALD:
Burial: July 07, 1921, Goose Cove Cemetery, St. Ann's Harbour, Victoria County, NS

More About ANGUS MACDONALD and CATHERINE MORRISON:
Marriage: Abt. 1870

Children of CATHERINE MORRISON and ANGUS MACDONALD are:
    i. Christy Effie⁵ MacDonald, b. North River, Victoria County, NS; m. Alexander 'Alex' MacDonald; b. North River, Victoria County, NS.

    Notes for Christy Effie MacDonald:
    This maybe the lady that raised Ella May (Pero) Oakley.

    Married first cousin - no children of their own.

    Notes for Alexander 'Alex' MacDonald:
    See notes on wife.

    ii. Catherine MacDonald, b. North River, Victoria County, NS.

3. NEIL⁴ MORRISON *(DONALD 'SPINNEY'³, NEIL² MORRISON*, BADDECK¹ MORRISON)* was born 1853 in Big Glen, Cape Breton County, NS. He married MOORES. She was born in Quebec.

Children of NEIL MORRISON and MOORES are:
  i. Alexander 'Alex'⁵ Morrison.
  ii. Archibald Niel 'Archie' Morrison, m. Elizabeth Ann MacArthur.

      Notes for Archibald Niel 'Archie' Morrison:
      These folks had 15 children.

  iii. Christena Jane Morrison, m. Stewart.

      Notes for Christena Jane Morrison:
      According to Ross files she either had 75 or 15 children

  iv. Donald Morrison.

      Notes for Donald Morrison:
      A military veteran.

  v. Hugh Morrison, d. Manitoba; m. Pearl

      Notes for Hugh Morrison:
      resided in Manitoba

  vi. John 'Jack' Morrison, d. 1937, Saskatchewan.

      Notes for John 'Jack' Morrison:
      never married

  vii. Laura Morrison, b. Kempt Head, Victoria County, NS; d. November 16, 1921, Man O War Point, Victoria County, NS.
  viii. Milton Morrison.
  ix. Nathaniel Morrison.

4. MURDOCH⁴ MORRISON *(DONALD 'SPINNEY'³, NEIL² MORRISON*, BADDECK¹ MORRISON)* was born 1859 in Big Glen, Cape Breton County, NS, and died in Big Glen, Cape Breton County, NS. He married ISABELLA 'BELLA' BUCHANAN, daughter of MURDOCH BUCHANAN and CHRISTINA MACLEOD.

79

Children of MURDOCH MORRISON and ISABELLA BUCHANAN are:
  i. Daniel⁵ Morrison, d. Big Baddeck, Victoria County, NS; m. Christine Ross; b. Sydney Mines, Cape Breton County, NS; d. Big Baddeck, Victoria County, NS.
  ii. Dollie Morrison, d. Boston, MA; m. Neil MacLennan, b. Grand River, Richmond County, NS.

      Notes for Dollie Morrison:
      Resided in Boston.

      Notes for Neil MacLennan:
      Maybe the Neil MacLennan that appears on the Newton Presbyterian Church WWI memorial in Boston.

  iii. John Morrison.

      Notes for John Morrison:
      Resided in Indian Brook, Victoria County, NS. Never married.

6. iv. Lena 'Lexie' Morrison, b. Abt. 1896, Big Baddeck, Victoria County, NS.
7. v. Tena Morrison, d. Boston, MA.

5. ALEXANDER 'SPINNEY'⁴ MORRISON *(DONALD 'SPINNEY'³, NEIL² MORRISON*, BADDECK¹ MORRISON)* was born 1845 in Big Glen, Cape Breton County, NS, and died in Big Glen, Cape Breton County, NS. He married MARGARET 'MAGGIE' MACLEOD, daughter of CHRISTOPHER MACLEOD and SARAH MORRISON. She was born Abt. 1854, and died in Big Glen, Cape Breton County, NS.

Notes for MARGARET 'MAGGIE' MACLEOD:
See Pg 118 of Bill Lawson notes (not available)

More About MARGARET 'MAGGIE' MACLEOD:
Date born 2: Abt. 1854, Baddeck Bay, Victoria County, NS

Children of ALEXANDER MORRISON and MARGARET MACLEOD are:

MORRISON GENEALOGY

FROM NEIL Morrison 1st cousin to
Daniel Murdock 'Spinney' Morrison
Prepared and researched by Shawna Morrison

Neil Morrison m. Annie MacDonald

Children:
Mary Morrison

b 1796 in Strond, Isle of Harris, Scotland
d 1881 in Big Glen, Victoria County, Cape Breton, Nova Scotia
Married Allan Morrison in 1819 Hebrides, Scotland

Children:
1a	Neil
1b	Malcolm (b Oct 10 1819 - Isle of Harris) m. Sarah Morrison
1c	Catherine (b 1822 – Isle of Harris) (d 1886)
1d	Kenneth (b 1823 – Isle of Harris)
1e	Roderick (b 1824 – Isle of Harris) (d Feb 21 1900) m. Christy
1f	John Allan (b July 17 1828 – Bouldarderie, CB, NS) (d May 19 1913) m. Sarah Maclean
1g	Christina (b 1835 – Upper Baddeck, Victoria Cty, CB, NS)
1h	Effie (b 1839 – Middle River, CB, NS)

Donald J. Morrison
b 1810 – Strond, Isle of Harris, Scotland
d in Big Baddeck, Cape Breton, Nova Scotia, Canada

Married Christy Shaw (b Sept 20 1820 – North Gut, Victoria Cty, CB NS)

Children:
- 2a   Annie
  (b May 1843 – Big Glen, Victoria Cty, CB, NS)
  (d Nov 2 1926) Buried: Goose Cove Cemetery, St. Ann's Bay, Victoria Cty, CB, NS
- 2b   Alexander

  (b 1845 – Big Glen, Victoria Cty, CB, NS) (d – Big Glen, CB, NS)
  Married Margaret Macleod (b 1854) (d – Big Glen, CB, NW)

  Children:
  - 2b.1   Mary
    (b – Baddeck Bay, Victoria, CB, NS)
    Married Kenneth Mackenzie

  - 2b.2   Margaret "Maggie"
    (b – Nova Scotia) (d Boston, Mass. USA)

- 2c   Catherine "Kate"
  (b 1847 – Big Glen, Victoria Cty, CB, NS) (d Sept 15 1885)
  Buried: Goose Cove Cemetery, St. Ann's Bay, Victoria, CB, NS)
  Married Angus MacDonald (b Aug 10 1840 – North River, Victoria, CB, NS)
  (d July 7 1921) Buried: Goose Cove Cemetery, St. Ann's Bay, CB, NS

  Children:
  - 2c.1   Christy "Effie"
    b Nov 10 1881 – North River, Victoria, CB, NS)
    Married Alexander MacDonald

2c.2   Catherine "Kate"
b March 1 1884 – North River, Victoria, CB, NS)

2d   Sarah
(b 1851 – Big Glen, Victoria Cty, CB, NS) (d Jan 4 1946)
Married Malcolm Maclean

2e   Neil Archibald
(b Oct 31 1853 – Big Glen, Victoria Cty, CB, NS)
(d May 11 1912 – Kaleida, Manitoba)
Buried: Archibald Cemetery, Manitou, Manitoba

(Rural Municipality of Pembina)

Neil was a young man in his early twenties when he moved to Quebec for work. There, he met and married Matilda Moores, and started a family. After their third child, they moved to Kenora, Ontario, where he worked as a contractor with the CP Rail to blast rock. Neil, being the supervisor for his crew, resigned from CPR after grieving the loss of one of his workers when an explosion occurred. Just after their fourth child was born (my great grandfather, Archibald), they moved onto farmland in Kaleida, Manitoba, where he began his career as a farmer. Around 1903, he donated his land for the Kaleida townsite, and for a part of the CPR line to run through it, which ran from Darlingford. Their neighbours, friends and some of Matilda's family members from Quebec joined them in Kaleida, forming a larger community of farmers. Neil and Matilda opened their house to be Kaleida's Post Office, where people would mail their letters and remain visiting all the day through. Neil rode his horse, Neil Gow, to deliver the mail to where it needed to go. Neil also helped to find employment to many immigrants who arrived around the area.

Married Matilda Zilpha Moores Aug 12 1873
(b Aug 22 1851 – Matapedia, Quebec)
(d Feb 21 1937 – Manitoba)
Buried: Archibald Cemetery, Manitou, Manitoba
(Rural Municipality of Pembina)

Children:

2e.1   Christina "Tina"
                 (b 1875 – Quebec) (d – Western USA)

m. William Stevenson

2e.2 Donald
(b Nov 16 1876 – Quebec)
(d Aug 19 1924 – Kaleida, Manitoba)
m Annabelle Anderson

2e.3 Nathaniel
(b July 29 1878 – Quebec)
(d March 17 1925 – Kaleida) – never married

2e.4 Archibald Neil - my g grandfather
(b March 18 1881 – Kenora, Ontario)
(d July 30 1962 – Dundurn, Saskatchewan)
m Elizabeth Ann McArthur

2e.5 John "Jack" Thomas
(b March 4 1883 – Kaleida, Manitoba)
(d May 24 1938) – never married

2e.6 Laura Madeline
(b Sept 20 1886 – Kaleida, Manitoba)
(d Jan 11 1928 – New Ulm, Minnesota USA)
m Heine "Henry" Neuwirth

2e.7 Alexander
(b Sept 15 1888 – Kaleida, Manitoba)
(d 1935 – Dundurn, Saskatchewan)
m Mae Young

2e.8 Milton Irvine
(b June 25 1890 – Kaleida, Manitoba)
(d Feb 28 1972 – Kaleida, Manitoba) – never married

2e.9 Hugh Borthwick
(b Dec 16 1872 – Kaleida, Manitoba)
(d Jan 9 1957 – Kaleida, Manitoba)
m Carolyne McBean

2f Mary
(b 1857 – Big Glen, Victoria Cty, CB, NS)
(d – South Cove, Little Narrows, CB, NS)

Married Henry MacIver (b 1856 – South Cove, CB, NS)
(d 1901 – Louisburg, CB, NS)
(buried: Little Narrows Presbytarian Church, Victoria Cty, CB, NS)

Children:

f.1		James C. (b July 6 1879 – Joggins Mines, Cumberland, CB, NS) (d Feb 14 1907) m Margaret Buchanan
2f.2		Murdoch (b 1881 – Southside, Little Narrows, CB, NS) (d 1886)
2f.3		John Charlie (b Dec 20 1885 – Southside, Little Narrows, CB, NS)
2f.4		Lorena (b Nov 15 1887 – Southside, Little Narrows, CB, NS)
2f.5		Christena (b Oct 20 1894 – Southside, Little Narrows, CB, NS)
2f.6		Daniel John (b June 20 1897 – Washabuck, Victoria Cty, CB, NS) d Aug 12 1918)
2g		Murdoch J. (b 1859 – Big Glen, Victoria Cty, CB, NS) (d June 9 1939 – Big Glen, Victoria Cty, CB, NS) (buried: St. Andrews United, Baddeck Forks, CB, NS) Married Isabella "Sadie" Buchanan (b Jan 1860 – Nova Scotia) (d 1915) (buried: St. Andrews United, Baddeck Forks, CB, NS)

Children:
2g.1 Daniel Murdoch
(b Nov 15 1891 – Nova Scotia)
(d 1967 – Big Baddeck, CB, NS)
m (1) Christine Ross (b 1886 – Sydney Mines,

Appendix B – Daisy Delinger McEachen Genealogy

Daisy's father: CHARLES ALEXANDER JULIEN MCEACHEN
Born: Parish of Portland, County of Dorset, England, baptized June 6, 1858 in Church of England.

His father JOHN MCEACHEN, born Scotland 1825, died 2 April 1890 age 66 (1861 England Census).

His mother: ANGELIQUE SPLINGARD, marriage 10 Feb 1851 – they had three children:

JOHN MCEACHEN, born1853; FELISTEE MCEACHEN, born 1856; and CHARLES.
Charles married on 17 June 1878, at St. Mary Magdalene, Woolwich, Kent, Greenwich, England to ALICE MARTIN SAVILLE (name on NY birth report for Minnie).
They moved (after marriage and after Maud was born) in 1880 to Brooklyn, New York. There, Charles Alexander worked as some kind of inspector, living at 771 Bergen Street, Brooklyn in 1886 when daughter Minnie was born. In 1882, when son Alexander was born, he was a waiter living at 276 Washington Street, Brooklyn, NY. Daisy was born in 1884.
Alice's father's name was MATTHEW SAVILLE. The 1891 Canada Census shows Alice's religion as Baptist. Alice's information on the 1871 England Census shows her age as 14. Her father is shown as Matthew Saville, cabinet maker, age 44, and her mother as Mary A. E. Saville, age 34.
Alice's father Matthew married at age 34; her mother Mary Alice Elizabeth Saville (nee Chaplanden) age 28; sister Lavinia, age 10; brother Harvey, age 4; sister Matilda, age 2; and brother Henry, age 1 month on the 1861 English Census. On the 1871 census, records show: Alice, 14; Kenny, age 14; Matilda, age 12; Henry, age 10; Caroline, age 8; Edward, age 6; Alfred age 4, and another Alfred, age 3 days. Also, a Caroline Chaplanden, age 26 (sister of Alice's mother), is listed.
In April of 1891, some of the Saville family was in Nova Scotia (see 1891 census); except their father, who died around 1872 in England.
Daisy's brother and sisters:

MINNIE SANFORD MCEACHEN:
Born March 4,1886, Brooklyn, Kings, New York: information from New York births and christenings, 1640-1962 and 1891 Canada Census.
5 years old, 1891 Canada Census.
Religion: Baptist, Living in Halifax, Nova Scotia.
Minnie disappears from the ancestry records after her parent's deaths in 1894.

DAISY (DAISY DELINGER MCEACHEN):
Born in Brooklyn, New York in 1884. When she was 7 years old, 1891 Census Canada shows her in Halifax, Nova Scotia. At age 17 in 1901, the census reports: Living as a domestic with Lownds family in Halifax, NS.
Birthplace England. (incorrect on the record by choice or census error)
Religion: Church of England.
Mr. Lownds was a plumber at the time. Son Frank E C Lownds, 18 years old. In the 1911 census, Daisy is still with the Lownds' but now Rebecca Lownds is head of the family and shown as widowed, age 65. Frank, age 25, still lives at home with Daisy, now age 26. Now she is shown as born in New Brunswick, the same as her employer, Rebecca, and with a birth date of Feb 1885.
Rebecca Lownds died on August 16, 1928. Her son Frank went on to marry Jessie Matilda Ellis on April 25, 1929.

ALEXANDER MCEACHEN:
Daisy's brother was 9 years old on the 1891 Census Canada. Alexander married Daisey M. Wirell (sometimes spelled Wirell, Wirrell or Wirrel) in Halifax (Dartmouth), daughter of Robert and Isabel Wirell, on 6 October, 1909, (age 29). Daisy Wirell was 18 at the time of marriage (born 1891).Church of England. Job shown as foreman ordnance in Halifax. Same as his Uncle Harvey Saville had been in 1894.
Witnesses at marriage were: Maud McEachen Wirell and Thomas Wirell who were married 31 august, 1901.Thomas was a polisher, listed as his work. His father Robert also shown as a polisher on the marriage record.
Alexander – Daisy Delinger McEachen's brother is shown on Nova Scotia death records as Charles Alexander McEachern. He died March 20, 1926 in Dartmouth, at age 44. Cause of death was pulmonary tuberculosis

ALICE MAUD MCEACHEN:
Born June 26, 1879, in England. Baptist Religion. From 1891 Canada Census: 11 years old. Charles Alexander McEachen, father, shown as photographer.

She married Thomas Wirell on August 31, 1909. They had one son, Thomas Gordon James Wirrell, born October 23, 1910, Dartmouth, NS. The 1891 census shows the entire McEachen family in Nova Scotia listed as of the Baptist religion. In England, Daisy's mother and father were born into the Anglican religion.

Appendix C – The Trial: Transcripts and Newspaper Reports

Excerpts from Testimony During Murder Trial Of Dan Murdock Morrison
May 28, 29, 30, and June 1, 1957

The Trial began after opening with swearing in of witness Alexander McLean. Mr. McLean had lived in Big Baddeck for 48 years and knew the accused, Dan Morrison, for probably 30 years. He knew Daisy since she came to Baddeck five or six years back. He lived about a mile from the accused's home. Between his home and the accused there was one other home owned by Murdock MacKay.
On February 2 Alex MacLean got a phone call from Dan Morrison asking him to come to Dan's house. That was 1:15 pm on February 2, 1957.

Alex MacLean's testimony:
"When I got there he was standing alone outside at the door of his house. No one else was present. I asked him what was wrong. He said "Daisy hung herself."

We went into the house through the kitchen. I saw Daisy Morrison hanging by the stairs in the hall. She was hanging to a rope, her back to the banister of the stairway. Her feet were about inches from the floor. An overturned chair was a couple of feet from Daisy's body. I stayed in the house about four or five minutes. He asked "what should I do?" and I told him the best thing was to get in touch with the doctor, so he did. He was on the phone to Dr. C.L. MacMillan when I left. Then I left and drove to Dan Neil MacMillan's to tell him what happened. His house is about a mile and a half from the Morrison home. I stayed there about 20 minutes and then returned to Morrison's with Dan Neil and his wife. When we got there Dr. MacMillan and Morrison were half way to the house from the main road. After Morrison phoned Dr. MacMillan and went to the road to meet him. We went to the house behind Dr. MacMillan and Morrison."

"When I got there Dr. MacMillan asked me if I would go back to the road and stop the RCMP, and I did. I then went back to the house to get Mr. MacMillan and his wife, and I took them home and I went to my home."

"There are three farms within a mile and a half going west they are Christopher MacLeod's, mine, Dan MacMillan's and a couple of vacant ones. Going east the closest is Neil MacKay about three miles from the Morrisons.

Dr. C.L. MacMillan's Testimony:

"I live and have practiced medicine in Baddeck and vicinity for 29 years, out of my home. On February 2nd I was in Sydney. I have known Dan Morrison for several years. After he called me on February 2nd I drove to his house and met him at his gate by the road. He was alone. I asked him what the trouble was. He told me his wife hung herself. I knew the deceased slightly. She had been to my office once.

We walked up the hill to the house because of the considerable snow. It was more than 300 yards from the gate to the farmhouse. On the walk up the incline I asked him about her mental condition, mental health, and he told me she has not been very good and he was coaxing her to go to see a doctor and she would not, and when he came home the night before she told him she took a dizzy spell and fell. He said he had been working that morning in the woods, cutting wood, and when he came home he found the door locked and no dinner ready and he thought she was upstairs and he opened the door and found her hanging in the hall. When he told me she had hung herself the first thing that came to mind was to ask him about her mental health. Generally something is wrong with a person when they hang themselves.

I found the remains of Mrs. Morrison hanging in the hall, back to the stairs with her feet five of six inches off the floor. I examined the body and found evidence of rigor mortis around the eyes and jaws and hands. In the rest of the body rigor mortis had not set in. I judged it was over three hours she had been dead – three or four.

When I first went into the house there was no one else. While I was there some people came in Dan MacMillan and his wife and Alex MacLean. No police were at the home, I went down the hill to meet the RCMP. I took no part in the autopsy that was performed by Dr. Gyorfi the pathologist from Sydney.

Dr. Gyorfi Testimony:

Excerpts from Court questioning Dr. Gyorfi on June 1, 1957, about his autopsy findings. He was a practicing physician and pathologist in Sydney for five years, at St. Rita's hospital, Sydney, St. Joseph's, Glace Bay and St. Elizabeth, North Sydney.

Dr. Gyorfi said "Autopsy was performed at Victoria County

Memorial Hospital at Baddeck. It took about two hours. In attendance were Dr. MacMillan, Sgt. Finney, Corporal Duff, Const. Tiller and the head nurse of the Baddeck hospital. One of the police officers took hand written notes dictated by me. I compiled my formal report after the autopsy."

    The doctor found a superficial cut over the left temporal area about one inch above the left-eye brow, with sharp edge, about three-quarters inch measurement. There was some dried blood over the temporal area and also on the hair, but not on any other part of the face. This shows that the body was in a horizontal position when bleeding occurred. Otherwise it would have run over the face.

    The tongue was swollen, protruding from the mouth, and bitten. There were two constriction marks, one quite deep, and a furrow surrounding the neck, situated a little bit above the Adam's apple. There was another about a half an inch below that first mark, much less pronounced, not indenting the skin, leaving only a superficial mark from the Adam's apple to the left side but not surrounding the neck.

    My conclusion was that the rope surrounding the neck cut the air passage and caused the protruding of the tongue and the swelling The rope cut off the circulation and respiration – no way for the blood to run out.

    In addition I found on the body, on both sides of the shoulders there was some ecchymosis which means blood dried under the skin, hematoma. Both legs were swollen due to gravity forcing the blood to the legs during hanging.

    The larynx, upper part of the throat, was completely compressed by the swelling of the different tissues. The Adam's apple was broken. There was quite extensive hemorrhaging under the skin surrounding the deep neck furrow. The ribs to the front of the body were fractured on both sides – 5th, 6th, 7th, 8th, 9th, 10th and 11th ribs were parted on both sides – seven on each side. The fracture line was a straight line – each rib was fractured above the other at about the same level, symmetrical. There was some blood around the fracture between the chest bone and the skin. The lower part of the left and right lung was congested, filled with blood. In the abdomen there was quite an extensive hemorrhage between the peritoneum, which is the covering of the bowel – the cause of that was the rupture of a small vessel which attached the gut with the body, and the right kidney was congested. I would say the bleeding lasted about a half-hour, and stopped at time of death."

Dr. Gyorfi was asked by the court if he had an opinion about the cause of the injury to the stomach. He said "I think it was caused by some external violence unknown to me. But I don't think it was caused by the rope."

The right kidney was congested, containing more blood than the left. There were some patches in the large vessels indicating advanced age of the deceased – sclerosis. That finding has no relation to the injuries. She was roughly 60 years of age[1]. There were also adhesions between the wall of the chest and the lungs indicating some inflammation unrelated to the injuries.

Court: " Death wasn't caused by any kidney condition?"

Witness: "No. There were some adhesions on both sides between the wall of the chest and the lungs indicating some inflammation. That also has no relation to the injuries."

When asked by the Court for his opinion about the injury to the ribs, Dr. Gyorfi replied: "I would think the deceased fell down and hit with her body some relatively large and relatively hard surface. I think this because the injury was so symmetrical. Also at the same time I found injuries to both shoulders."

Court: "The pattern of broken ribs was such that you came to the conclusion the person must have fallen down?"

Dr. Gyorfi: "face down."

Court: "And these injuries caused thereby?"

"Yes"

"Would an ordinary fall do that?"

"In relation to the age, yes. At that age the bones are not so strong and hard as in younger people and much less violence would cause fractures."

"Would the injuries to the ribs cause the death of the woman?"

"Definitely not."

"You say there were broken ribs on both sides?"

"Yes."

"Do you think a fall on the face against some hard object would cause the ribs to break on both sides of the body?"

"That is the only way I can imagine this to happen. It has been so symmetrical. Something pushed the chest wall and in that way they were broken."

"You think they were all broken at the same time?"

"Yes."

---

1   Daisy was born in 1884. Her true age in 1957 was 73, not 60.

"Could that have been caused by the victim falling on the floor?"

"Very hard to say. I doubt if a flat surface could cause that. It is hard to see how a flat surface would push the chest wall in."

Dr. Gyorfi's opinion was that the injuries were all inflicted before death and, in essence, he said they were consistent with Dan Murdoch's second statement taken by police on February 3rd, 1957:

"That about 8 a.m. the 2-2-57 while she was standing on the kitchen floor near the couch she called me a whore's bastard, that I pushed her and she lost her balance and fell against the corner of the couch striking her chest on the corner of the couch, and knocking herself out."

RCMP testimony:

Corporal A.L. Duff was a 15 year veteran of the RCMP stationed in Baddeck for the past four and a half years. He had been the first to arrive on the scene. He was acquainted with Dan Morrison. He told the Court in reply to questions:

"I received a telephone call with regard to a hanging that had taken place. I went to the home of Dan Murdoch Morrison and Dan Neil MacMillan and Mrs. MacMillan and Alexander MacLean were at the residence. As I proceeded to the home Dr. MacMillan and the late C.W.E McCurdy were present with me."

Q: "Did you enter the home?"
A: "yes"
Q: "Was the accused there?"
A: "yes"
Q: "Where?"
A: "In the kitchen in a rocking chair to the left of the kitchen stove."
Q: "Are you familiar with the house?"
A: "yes"
Q: "Describe the house."
A: "Two storey frame home. As you enter there was a small porch, a large kitchen, and off the kitchen was a bedroom, and to the right as you walked into the kitchen there was a doorway leading to the front hall, and a bit of a pantry to the left. On the right side of the hall was a dining room and to the left was a sitting room and a storeroom behind that. The stairs were in the hall that went to the second floor. As you proceeded upstairs there were two rooms on the right and two on the left."

Q: "When you entered the house what room did you enter?"
A: "The kitchen."
Q: "Tell us what you did."
A: "I entered with Dr. MacMillan and Mr. MacCurdy. The accused was sitting to the left of the stove and Mrs. MacMillan was seated on a couch and Dr. MacMillan in a chair. Alex MacLean came in and he was standing there. We were shown to the front hall, the door had been partly closed. Dr. MacMillan, Mr. MacCurdy and myself entered together and we found the remains of Daisy Morrison. Mrs. Daniel Morrison, hanging from a rope suspended from the banister on the second floor. Dr. MacMillan and I examined the remains and found she had been hanging for some time. Her hands were beginning to get stiff. Rigor mortis setting in."
Q: "What time was that?"
A: "Approximately quarter to three, half past two, on the 2nd of February, 1957. I noticed the rope from which she was suspended had stains which appeared to be blood, and considerable blood matted her hair. I also noticed there was a slipper off the deceased; and a chair was overturned on the floor."
Q: "how high were her feet off the floor?"
A: "Possibly an inch and a half or two inches. Just off the floor. There was a cut on the left temple of the deceased which I presumed had caused the blood in her hair. Her hands were clean. No sign of blood on them. She was fully clothed."
Q: "What about her face and neck?"
A: "The face was clean and quite pale. On her chest below her chin there was a spot of blood. The neck was clean in front and considerable blood down the back."
Q: "Any blood on her face?"
A: "No, not that I recall. I examined the remainder of the downstairs and found what I presumed to be blood stains on the floor and wall and treads of the steps. We continued upstairs and there was another spot of blood at the head of the stairs on the floor. There was what appeared to be blood stains on one of the banister rails. A half hitch had been tied to the end of the rope from which the body was suspended – a double half hitch. The rope had been wrapped around and tied to the banister and there was a loose end sticking out."
Q: "Did you examine the rope?"
A: "Yes, hemp, new except for the blood stains. There was a knot at the end of the rope on the second floor and a noose around

her neck had been made of a loop of the rope and drawn tight. I left the upstairs and came down and Dr. MacMillan and myself and Mr. MacCurdy came out and closed the door, and I asked Alex MacLean if he would mind staying and seeing that nobody entered the front hall, as I intended to go back to the car. I then spoke to Mr. Morrison and asked to have a few words with him and we went into the bedroom off the kitchen."

At this point in the trial the jury was asked to retire so the Court could discuss an issue of Law. After the jury left the Judge asked Cpl. Duff to continue.

"We went into the room off the kitchen, Mr. Morrison and I. My purpose at that time was to inquire as to his wife's health and to get particulars from him as to how he had found his wife and what possibly may have caused her to be in the position she was. I asked him about his wife and he said she had not felt very well; she had head aches and often became quite nervous and upset, usually due to her financial condition. I noticed at that time stains of what appeared to be blood on Mr. Morrison's clothing. I told him I was going to the road and I would be back shortly. I went to the main road and called Sydney for assistance and then returned to the house. When I returned Dan Neil MacMillan and his wife and Alex MacLean left and Mr. Morrison and I were left alone in the kitchen."

Judge asked: "What time in the afternoon would that be?"

"Approximately 3 or 3:15, a good half hour after I arrived when I left the house when I left the home and I was down at the car approximately twenty minutes. Around quarter to four when I returned to the house."

"At what time did you have some conversation with the accused?"

"Yes, I had. I talked to Mr. Morrison and asked him about his wife, and what he had been doing. I had considerable conversation. I asked him how long he had been home during the winter months. I advised him that in all probability there would be an inquest. I told him that I would like to have a statement, and I gave him the usual warning – you need not say anything. You have nothing to hope from any promise of favour; nothing to fear from any threat whether or not you say anything. Anything you do and say may be used as evidence against you."

Q: "He wasn't charged at that time?"

A: "No"

Q: "Did you entertain any thought at that time about charging him for any offence?"

A: "Yes, I thought it was the proper thing to give him the warning."

Reference STATEMENT Marked C/1

Mr. Harris MacDonald, for the Crown asked Cpl Duff:

Q: "Tell His Lordship just how you took this statement?"

A: "I asked Mr. Morrison questions and he would give me answers. I would then write it down and read it back and ask him if it was correct. When he stated they were I would continue with a further question until the statement was completed. I then read the whole statement over and asked him if there were any changes he wished to make."

Q: "Look at this C/1 [2], is that the statement you took from Morrison on the afternoon of February 2nd?"

A: "That is correct."

Q: "What happened after that?"

A: "We had a cup of tea. It was then six or six-fifteen."

Q: "Who made the tea?"

A: "Mr. Morrison."

Q: "Did you have a cup of tea?"

A: "Yes and at approximately six or shortly thereafter Const. Tiller and Const. Brooke arrived, and some time later, possibly half an hour or three-quarters of an hour later, Sgt. Finney arrived. I explained things to Const. Tiller and Sgt Finney as we went over the house and Const. Tiller and I took blood scrapings from the floor and we obtained the clothing from Mr. Morrison. Later on we removed the remains from the banister and they were taken to the Victoria County Hospital. We obtained the rope, and also another rope that was in the back room upstairs. There was a mop I took possession of, and two towels, a water bucket and several articles we felt might be required."

Q: "Did you later, either that day or the next, take another statement? Did you talk with the accused again?"

A: "Yes. I met him at one o'clock in the afternoon Sunday, the third of February, and went back to the home of the accused. We left Baddeck around one o'clock and went to Baddeck Forks, and Sgt. Finney and Const. Tiller and Const. Brooks and myself were there.

---

2   Statement of Daniel Murdock Morrison signed and dated February 2nd, 1957 at Baddeck Forks, NS.

Const. Tiller and myself continued investigation and later I had another conversation with the accused and shortly after that took another statement."

Q: "Between the taking of the first statement and the conversation you are talking about now, on the 3rd of February, had an autopsy been performed?

A: "Yes."

Q: "Had you been made aware of the results?"

A: "Yes. I attended the autopsy."

Q: "Where had the accused been?"

A: "He had been in Baddeck. He came in to Baddeck with us Saturday night, and we picked him up here at the court house at approximately one o'clock in the afternoon."

Q: "Where did he spend the night?"

A: "I believe he got a night's lodging in the County jail. Sgt Finney and I drove him back to his home. Sgt Finney, Const. Tiller and myself talked to Mr. Morrison for fifteen minutes or half an hour. We talked about the remarks he had made in the statement the previous day and that the warning still held good. He continued telling the same story he had previously told. There were some things that were not quite clear and we tried to have him clarify them.

He had told us he had not taken his saw to the woods of the previous day, and on the second day he told us he had brought it back. He clarified that by saying he had left it in the woods overnight. Const. Tiller asked him a question with regards to footprints about the house and some stains we found on the snow and he clarified that. He also maintained that he had been getting along well with his wife and when I suggested to him that they did not get along and that they had quarreled considerably he said yes, that is right. I had known the accused for the last two or three years.

I also pointed out things that I thought were inconsistent in the autopsy report and his statement, C/1, taken February 2nd. With regard to the autopsy I had learned that Mrs. Morrison had met her death by strangulation and that she had received a severe blow of some description on the chest that had caused considerable damage – bruises beneath the skin and laceration on the side of the head. We asked Mr. Morrison about these things and one remark he made was that his wife had fallen the day before on her face which would account for her bruised nose. At that time I could not understand the broken bones she had. He kept pretty well to the statement he had given the previous day – that he did not know what would cause her to do such a thing. We asked him to clarify the other bruises on her shoulders. I suggested they did not get along and had quarreled considerably and he agreed to that. Sgt. Finney asked why he had pushed her and he said they had a fight. Sgt. Finney asked where and he said "right there" and he pointed to the corner of the couch, and from then on he reenacted his actions the previous day. That was before the taking of the second statement.

He went into the front hall – he told us his wife was then unconscious, and he picked her up and carried her to the hall and sat her on a chair. He told me she had cursed him and he got cross and gave her a shove and she had fallen on the corner of the couch on the right side of the kitchen as you are facing the front of the house, to the right of the door as you entered. She lay on the floor unconscious and he picked her up and carried her to the front hall and put her on a kitchen chair and when he let her go she fell off the chair onto the floor and struck her head on a telephone insulator that had been used as a door stop, and that accounted for the blood on the temple.

I think Sgt. Finney asked him to show how he hanged his wife. He demonstrated with the remaining piece of rope how he had tied the knot and placed the noose around the neck of his wife. I was used as the victim and Sgt. Finney and Const. Tiller watched. He threw the rope over the banister and tied the knot after it had been drawn up a certain distance.

Mr. Morrison then went back into the kitchen and I gave the accused the second warning and told him I wanted to take a further statement. At that time he made another cup of tea and had a lunch while I took the second statement. He had lunch and Sgt. Finney and myself had a cup of tea. I mentioned to him that it was as a serious thing that he had harmed his wife and that she had died. I wanted him to know it was a serious matter. And that he might be charged.

During the second statement I asked the accused questions and he agreed to them. I would write it down and read it back. If I was not correct I would write it down the way he wished to have it written. After each question I would read it back to him. At the conclusion of the statement I read the whole statement back to him and asked if it was correct and if there were any changes he wanted to make and after completing the statement he signed it and we signed it and initialed all the pages."

Donald MacNeil, Dan Murdock Morrison's attorney continued cross examination of Cpl. Duff on Wednesday, May 29, 1957:

"Corporal, in your evidence yesterday you stated you arrived at the farm and walked up from the gate to the house in company with Dr. MacMillan and Mr. MacCurdy?"

"Yes."

"And when you arrived the accused was in the kitchen?"

"Yes."

"And at that time you examined the house and you described what you found?"

"Yes."

"You then took the accused into a room off the kitchen?"

"Yes."

"What did you ask the accused?"

"A few questions with regard to his wife's condition, how she had been in the past week or so, and he stated she had been very dizzy, having dizzy spells and severe headaches. I asked in regard to the time he had returned home, and when he had left home."

"What was his reply?"

"He inferred he left for work at approximately 8:30 a.m. and he arrived back between 1 and 1:30."

"You left then to summon help?"

"Yes."

"Then you returned and everybody left except yourself and the accused?"

"Yes."

"How long did you sit in the kitchen talking to him before you began to take the statement?"

"Approximately 20 minutes to a half an hour."

The remainder of Cpl. Duff's testimony was the same as he told to the prosecutor earlier during the trial. Dan's attorney, Mr. MacNeil was trying to determine the timing of the second interview on February 3 and what if anything had occurred to influence the accused to agree to sign a second statement admitting to causing Daisy's death by hanging. Mr. MacNeil asked specifically what aspects of statement C/1 cannot be true because of the autopsy findings.

Cpl. Duff replied: "The fact that he only went as far as he did in his statement – he did not tell the complete story as to the time he left his home and when he returned and what he had done. We questioned him in regard to his movements."

Mr. MacNeil asked: "You advised the accused that due to the autopsy report the contents of the first statement (C/1) could not be true. What in C/1 could not be true in view of the autopsy report? Could not C/1 be true and the autopsy report be true?"

"Yes, that is possible."

"When was the accused put under formal arrest?"

"Sunday evening some time after six o'clock, on February 3rd."

"With regard to the taking of the second statement, C/2. As I understand it you had a conversation with the accused around four o'clock. He told you something and then he enacted the scene and then C/2 was taken?"

"Yes. At approximately four it was explained to the accused that he had been warned the previous day and that there were things we wanted to clarify and we talked for approximately twenty minutes and then he reenacted the scene and then the second statement was taken, around four-thirty."

"When you say he repeated what he had told you in C/1, the whole of it?"

"Up to a point."

Prosecution, Mr. MacDonald, raised an objection.

Mr. MacNeil continued examining Cpl. Duff.

"How was Morrison talking at that time? Was he talking slowly or fast?"

"Talking in a very normal way."

Objection by prosecutor.

"Talking in a very normal way?"

Objection.

"Tell me his manner of speaking?"

"Quite his usual manner, soft spoken. He was quite a soft spoken person; did not talk a great deal, but carried on a good conversation."

"While we were talking to him with regard to the first statement, C/1, and we got to the point of how he got along with his wife and I asked him if it wasn't a fact that they did not get along at all and his reply was yes. I then said "In fact, Mr. Morrison, you and your wife quarreled considerably and he agreed to that. Sgt. Finney than asked why he had pushed her and Mr. Morrison replied that they had been in a heated argument and quarrelling and she cursed him and he shoved her. Sgt. Finney then asked him where, where he had pushed her, and he pointed to the position Sgt. Finney was in and said "right there".

"Where was he?"

"Sitting at the corner of the couch in the kitchen on a chair. The lower front corner of the couch was at his back. Mr. Morrison continued then to tell the story of what happened."

Mr. MacNeil continued "Look at C/1, the last paragraph, 'The farm is in my name and I look after it and keep the house going. My wife was always good to get the meals on time, but today when I got home there was no dinner ready – we always got along well and never had any quarrels'. I take it you were challenging C/1? Objection by prosecution!

(Page 65 – transcript)

Sgt F.H. Finney, RCMP Sydney, sworn and examined by Mr. MacDonald, prosecution.

Q: "After you completed your investigation of the home of the accused on 2nd February 1957 where did you go?"

A: "Baddeck, at 8:30pm or thereabouts. The accused went with me partly on my suggestion and partly on his own.

After I got to the home of the accused I assisted Corporal Duff to commence an investigation into the death of Mrs. Morrison. Before leaving I asked the accused if he would like to come to Baddeck or stay in his own home and he said he would sooner come to Baddeck.

He was not under arrest at this time. Only he and myself were in the car. I took him to the RCMP Detachment. We chatted along the way. I took no statement from him at that time."

Q: "What happened to the accused that evening?"

A: "He had no place to stay in Baddeck and I asked if he wanted to go home and he said he would sooner not and I asked if he had any money to pay for lodging in Baddeck and he said no he had not. I suggested I might be able to get him lodging in the County Jail and he said that would suit him fine.

When we got to the jail I knocked at the door. The jailer came to the door and I explained to him that Mr. Morrison was with me, and that he was not under arrest but I would like to have lodging for him for the night and the jailer agreed. I went into the corridor with him and left him at the jail with the jailer.

The next day at approximately one-thirty Corporal Duff and myself came to the County Jail to get Mr. Morrison. I went first and told the jailer we wanted to take Mr. Morrison to his home. We went into the jail and Mr. Morrison was in the corridor. The jailer opened the door and Mr. Morrison came our and came with us to his home.

After getting to the home of the accused he started a fire and sat down by the stove, and Const. Tiller, Corporal Duff and myself looked around the premises to see what we could see, and Const. Brook I detailed to proceed to the neighbours and see what they might know in regard to the incident. Constable Brook left. For approximately two hours we looked around the house and yard and finally we went into the kitchen – the three of us and Mr. Morrison were in the kitchen.

While we were looking around the accused was in the kitchen by the stove. He lit a fire and kept it going because it was very cold that day.

Sgt. Finney continued: Mr. Morrison was sitting at the end of the stove and I sat down almost in front of the stove and put my feet in the oven. Const. Tiller sat at the table on the angle to Mr. Morrison, and Const. Duff was in the vicinity of where I was. I said to the accused "The autopsy on your wife has been completed, and there are a few points I would like to get cleared up.

In the first place, the autopsy showed that she had some internal injuries including broken ribs, and that she died from being hanged, asphyxiation." Corpl. Duff told Mr. Morrison that he had given a statement to him the previous day and if there was anything he wished to change it would be perfectly in order to do it. At that time I was under the impression that Mrs. Morrison had either fallen or been pushed from the front stairs of the house and with that in mind I said to Mr. Morrison "Did you push her?" And he said "well, you fellows have treated me pretty fairly, I will tell you the whole story. Yes. I pushed her."

I asked why did he push her and he said "I was having my breakfast – and as a consequence of an argument with my wife the previous night, she was screaming at me and finally made a remark and called me a 'whore's bastard' and with that I more or less lost my head and pushed her."

He said she struck the couch which was in the corner of the kitchen close to where he was sitting. He showed us where. He stated that she fell on the floor unconscious and he then picked her up and carried her to the hall where it was cooler and seated her on a chair and she fell off the chair and struck her head on a telephone insulator that was on the floor; and then he thought she was suffering, and he did not want to see her suffer, and he went upstairs to where he knew there was some rope he had used for lines. He cut a piece off and came down and placed it around her neck and hanged her to the banister. I then asked if he would show us how he had done it.

All this time the statement was oral – nothing was written down. He readily showed us how he had done it. He got up from the table and made the motion of pushing his wife. Corpl. Duff acted the part of his wife and he showed us how she had struck the couch and how he had taken her into the hall and sat her on the chair and how she had fallen off and where the insulator was and how he had gone upstairs and got the rope and he showed the kind of knot he had made and the other piece of rope he had cut it off. He put it around her neck and pulled it snug and walked up the stairs holding the rope and pulled it over the banister and tied it, and showed us the kind of knot he tied and it was similar to the know that was in the rope holding Mrs. Morrison.

And then we returned to the kitchen. Corpl. Duff gave him the usual warning. He reminded him that he had been warned the day previously and the warning still stood, and after that he gave him the warning "You need not say anything. You have nothing to hope from any promise of favour and nothing to fear from any threat whether or not you say anything. Anything you say may be used in evidence against you."

Constable Tiller was still in the kitchen at that time and he asked Mr. Morrison about some tracks in the snow leading to a shed and he explained that these tracks were made by him on a previous occasion when he was looking for a shovel but he did not get it because the door was frozen shut. He then asked him about some stains in the snow behind the shed and Mr. Morrison told him that they were stains from where he had emptied the slop pail. Const. Tiller left then and went to the police car and that left Corpl. Duff and myself and Mr. Morrison in the kitchen. Cpl. Duff told Mr. Morrison we were going to take down in writing anything he would say, in other words, take another statement. Mr. Morrison was quite agreeable. Corpl. Duff did the questioning and writing down of the statement. The statement was taken by questions and answers. Cpl. Duff would ask Mr. Morrison a question and write it down and read the answer and ask Mr. Morrison if it was right and he would say it was right or it wasn't right.

Before the statement was completed Cpl. Tiller returned to the kitchen. He took no further part in the questioning. He walked through the kitchen and remained in the other part of the house. Shortly before he completed his statement Const. Duff read it over and explained it was his statement and asked if he wanted to make any changes; if so it was quite in order for him to do so, Mr. Morrison said it was correct and he signed it, and corpl. Duff and myself signed it as witnesses. This is statement C/2

The Court now questions the witness Sgt Finney, RCMP Officer in Charge of the investigation.

"You read the statement C/1?"

"Yes, sir."

"And you came to the conclusion it wasn't right?"

"That is right. It was signed by Mr. Morrison, and it said in the statement that he had been cautioned by Cpl. Duff."

"And you deemed that to be sufficient?"

"That is right."

"Just to be a little more sure –"

Referring to C/2: "Since I gave that statement I have had considerable conversation with the police and I understand that the warning given me by Corporal Duff yesterday and previously referred to still holds good with regard to anything that I may have said to the police and anything that I am about to say regarding the death of my wife Daisy... At no time have any of these police officers mistreated me, threatened me, promised me anything or held out any inducements to me. And anything I have said or am about to give in this statement is voluntary and of my own free will."
Mr. Morrison agreed with the following statement: "During the past four years at least my wife and I have not been getting along at all.."

Court: "The gist of what he told you was that he and his wife were not getting along well and they had a lot of squabbles. Did he tell you what the arguments could be about?"

Sgt Finney answered: "I recall one thing he said, arguments about money."

"Anything else?"

"Yes, he said she wasn't a wife to him."

"That is all contained in the Statement?"

"Yes."

"Did he tell you any other reasons for these arguments?"

"Yes. One other thing he mentioned was that she was always comparing him to her first husband[3] and belittling him in the light of her first husband."

"Did he tell you of any other sources of argument?"

"That is all I recall at the moment."

Court asks: "She was always after me about various things

---

3   First husband was William Leadley to whom she had been married for 20 years. He died in 1934 in Halifax, NS.

and made life miserable in general. She had gone as far as to say she would get me sent to the asylum if it was the last thing she would do on this earth?"

"Yes."

"Did he tell you why she would make a remark like that?"

"To get rid of him."

"What else did he tell you in regard to the questions that brought about these disclosures?"

"That is all."

"I met my wife through a lonely heart club in 1949 or 1950 and we were married in July or August 1950. I married her because I wanted companionship and a housekeeper. However, she was never a wife to me. Would you relate to the jury the gist of the conversation which brought this out?"

"He was asked where he met his wife and how come he married her."

"Through correspondence. He advertised in the paper and met her through that."

"Then he was asked why did he marry her?"

"That is right, and he said he wanted a housekeeper and somebody for companionship."

"Did he elaborate what he meant?"

"Yes. He said he was living alone in his house and it wasn't very good living alone, and he wanted somebody to look after the house and cook and be a companion."

"During the period we were married life was far from pleasant and at times was hell on earth?"

"Yes."

Source: (Pages 123-124 – court transcripts)

"Did he explain to you what he meant?"

"The continual fighting and squabbling between him and his wife. During the last three or four weeks due to his wife's nagging I could not sleep and stayed awake half the night, oftentimes hearing two and three o'clock striking and during the day could not do my work in the woods and hated to come home for dinner or my meals"?

"That is right."

"What brought that about?"

"Just continuing to tell us that he and his wife did not get along; life was a hell on earth."

"Because of her nagging?"

"That is right, and the arguments."

"Did he tell you the basis of her nagging other than the comparison with her first husband?"

"They did not get along. That is the only reason I recall. Went from bad to worse."

Judge asked: "Referring to C/1, he said 'since the last two years she has had bad headaches...she had loaned $100 to Murdock MacKay and she was worried that she would not get it back.' Wasn't that the basis?"

Sgt. Finney responded: "Partially. She had some money from her previous marriage; more than the accused had and she was lending it to Murdock MacKay and also to the accused; she had paid a considerable amount for work around the house and purchased a car and various things; and her having more money than he had kind of put him – well, he wasn't in the driver's seat. She had all the money.[4]"

"The accused related all this to you?"

"That is right."

"Did he also relate to you the comparison she would make between him and her first husband?[5]"

"He was everything that was good and the accused just could not live up to it."

(Page 125 – transcript):

Court: "Just after she got up and before she had her breakfast, about 8 a.m. Saturday, February 2nd, while she was standing on the kitchen floor near the couch she called me a 'whore's bastard'. I pushed her and she lost her balance and fell against the corner of the couch striking her chest on the corner of the couch and knocking herself out."

"Yes."

"Keeping me awake with her screaming, shouting, cursing and swearing. What brought that about?"

Finney: "He was telling us they were having an argument the previous night and he went to bed at eleven and she stood in the door way – his bedroom is off the kitchen – and shouted and screamed at him from eleven till one o'clock."

"Did he tell you what happened?"

---

4 This insight by the RCMP Officer gets to the central issue between Daisy and Dan.
5 Her first husband was Frederick Leadley, to whom she had been married for 20 years until he died at age 73 in hospital of natural causes.

"It was at that time she told him she would have him put in the asylum."

"Is that the time she was cursing and swearing?"

"That is right."

"Did he disclose to you the nature of the cursing and swearing?"

"No. He did not."

"Did he disclose to you the circumstances of her coming down? Did he tell you he got up and made the fire and prepared breakfast?"

"His breakfast."

"And then he called his wife?"

I don't recall that he called her. I think she just came down herself, and as soon as she got in the kitchen she started where she had left off the previous night, and a few minutes after that she called him a whore's bastard."

"And that is when he pushed her?"

"That is right. He said 'I picked her up and carried her to the front hall where it was cooler, and sat her on a kitchen chair. After I placed her on the chair she fell off sideways and fell on the floor striking the left side of her head on a telephone insulator that was on the floor. This cut her head and caused a lot of bleeding. I left her laying on the floor in the hall on her back with her head in a pool of blood. When I saw her laying on the floor suffering I lost my presence of mind and went upstairs to where I knew there was a rope and I cut a piece off with my pocket knife."

Did he say to you 'I lost my presence of mind'?

"My impression was that at that time he said he felt sorry for her and did not want to see her suffer."

Court asks: "Did he use the words "I lost my presence of mind"?

That was Corporal Duff's phrasing, which he agreed to.

"Can you recall the accused saying he lost his presence of mind?

"Not in those particular words. If I remember correctly he said he went out of his mind or off his head.

Do you know what he meant by that?

As far as I know he lost his presence of mind. That is what I got from it.

The Court asked "In any event you recall there were some words used like went off his head or out of his mind?

That is correct.

The meaning the accused conveyed to Corpl Duff and to you was put in the statement in the language "presence of mind" – that meant that he was out of his head or out of his mind?

That is correct.

The court then proceeded to read aloud the phrasing in sections of C/2 statement by Dan Murdock and then to question Sergeant Finney about police and accused verbal interaction during the taking and writing of the statement that Mr. Morrison signed voluntarily.

The Court questioning was followed by re-examination by Mr. MacDonald, prosecutor. Again it was about statement C/2.

Later, Const. Chris Tiller was sworn and examined by Mr. MacDonald. Cpl Tiller was attached to the RCMP identification branch which includes taking photographs of the scene, processing them and making prints and sketches. Cpl Tiller reviewed and explained all the photographic and sketch exhibits with the Court.

There was a five minute recess, after which Tiller was questioned about two small bottles marked C/13 and C/14. These contained scrapings of reddish substances from the stairs and the floor. Also he was questioned about other evidence that he had collected.

Mr. MacDonald asked him if he was present on the 3 February when the accused made a statement. Constable Tiller replied that he was present and was asked to tell the Judge and Jury the circumstances.

"We returned to the Morrison home, arrived there during the afternoon about 1:30 or 2:00 p.m. Cpl. Duff, the accused, Sgt. Finney and myself. We carried on a further investigation and I examined the foot prints outside the building, and some reddish stains behind the barn. Sgt. Finney, Cpl Duff and myself were in the kitchen with the accused. At that time the results of the autopsy was made known to the accused. Cpl Duff reminded him he had been warned the previous day and that the warning still stood. The accused indicated that he knew that, and for possibly fifteen minutes he said his previous statement was correct. Corpl Duff then said in effect, "Actually you did not get along with your wife" and the accused agreed. Corpl Duff then said "You were fighting most of the time", and the accused agreed to that. Sgt. Finney then asked where did he push her and he indicated that he had pushed her towards the couch in the kitchen.

He was then asked if he would show us how it happened and he did.

The Court asked: Looking at these exhibits, pictures of the house. Everything looks very neat and tidy.

Cpl, Tiller replies "A very neat home."

"Is that the way you found it?"

"Yes, my Lord, very neat."

Mr. MacDonald recalled Cpl. Duff.

"At the time the Jury retired you were telling us you had taken the accused into a room?"

"That is correct."

"Look at these exhibits and tell us which room the accused was taken into."

"The bedroom off the kitchen, shown C/6."

"Pick up the narrative from there and tell us what happened?"

"I went into the bedroom with the accused and asked a few questions relating to his wife's health and condition and when he had returned and found the remains."

"At that time there was just you and the accused?"

"The accused and I were in the room together."

"Had any other member of the Force arrived at that time?"

"No."

"Were there any other people there?"

"Yes. Mr. and Mrs. Dan Neil MacMillan and Alexander McLean. We talked for a short time in the bedroom and then returned to the kitchen and the accused sat beside the stove again. I left Mr. MacLean to see that nobody entered the front of the house and I left and went to the road around 3 o'clock."

Corporal Duff was then asked to read the Statement C/1 in Court aloud which he did.

It read in part: ". . . I am a married man and have been living with my wife at Baddeck forks off and on for the past six years. I am sixty-five years of age and my wife was about four years younger than I am. She had been previously married to a man by the name of Fisher who lives at the Pier in Sydney. Her maiden name was Dillinger and had been brought up in Halifax, N.S.[6]

"My wife and I were married in the month of August, 1950, and she lived at Baddeck Forks ever since. I have worked away quite a lot and last winter I worked in Baddeck until the month of October and then did a few jobs around until December, 1956, when I returned home and started cutting pulp. I have been cutting pulp alone

---

6   Her first husband was Frederick Leadley, to whom she had been married for 20 years until he died at age 73 in hospital of natural causes.

for the past week or so off and on and have cut about five cord. My wife has been living at home all the time except when she would go for a visit to Sydney. She had no relatives that she knew of but visited friends in the Pier District. She had a house in Sydney that she was selling and she was having a bit of trouble getting her monthly payments. Since the last two years she has headaches she wouldn't go to the doctor. She became very nervous and would get upset over little things..."

The morning of the argument, February 2, he said she had fallen on the couch and struck her chest and she knocked herself out. He demonstrated it for us how he had pushed her. He pointed out that when she cursed at him he got cross and shoved her.

Did you examine the couch?

Yes, I did.

There was a mattress on it. It is an old fashioned kitchen couch; quite hard, the horse-hair type. It was covered with a rug over the edge. Underneath the rug was quite hard wood.

"At what time did you ask the accused where his bedroom was?"

"When I first entered?"

"Yes?"

"No."

"Did you ask him at all?"

"I asked him some time later on where he and his wife slept."

He slept in the bedroom by the kitchen. His wife slept upstairs.

Mr. MacNeil continued questioning asking Corpl Duff about the autopsy results and the first statements. He asked "Is it not true that both statements C/1 and C/2 could have been true and the findings of the autopsy report accurate?

Cpl. Duff answered "The autopsy report was accurate. I took the statement C/1 from the accused which I did not believe; but it could have been true. I informed the accused by referring to the great number of broken ribs and to a bruise on his wife. The broken ribs I felt had been caused from a blow, pressure on the sternum.
I asked him how she had obtained these injuries and he replied his wife had fallen the day before and hit her nose on the floor and her nose had bled. As to the broken ribs, he did not give any answer as to the cause. He said he had no idea how she had obtained them. He maintained the contents of C/1 for about fifteen minutes.

On February 3 after the autopsy report, Sgt. Finney asked him

"Why did you push your wife and the accused stated his wife had cursed him, and Sgt Finney asked where he had pushed her and he said, "Right there" – where Sgt Finney was sitting.

On Feb 3, he said "During the past few years my wife and I have not been getting along at all. During the last two years I have not been home as I was working away and only home on week-ends now and again. This winter I have been home steady since before Christmas and y wife and I have had considerable trouble with the arguments getting stronger as time went on. She was always after me about various things."

Court: "Did he explain to you what these arguments were about?

"Yes. He stated some of them were over money."

"Did he give you any other reasons?"

"Another was that they never went out together. She accused him of going and not taking her."

Court asks: "Anything with reference to her previous husband?"

Sgt Duff replied "Very little mention of her previous husband. I asked who she had been married to and he knew very little about it."

"Did he say she would compare him with her previous husband?"

"I don't recall right off hand."

"She was always after me about various things and made life miserable in general. She had gone so far as to say she would get me sent to the asylum if it was the last thing she should do." What did the accused say that led to you put that in the statement?"
Answer: "She had gone as far as to say she would get him sent to the asylum if it was the last thing she would do on earth." Those were practically his own words. She told him she would drive him crazy."

Question: "Did he say how?"

Answer: "No, he did not say."Just related things that happened."

Question: "She had told him she was going to drive him crazy?"

"Yes, practically his own words."

Question: "I met my wife through a lonely hearts club...however...I married her because I wanted companionship and a housekeeper. However, she was never a wife to me?"

Answer: "he wanted companionship on the farm; wanted

somebody with him to look after the home."

Question: "She was never a wife to me." Would you look at C/12 and point out the bedroom Mrs. Morrison occupied?"

Answer: "The bedroom to the right of the stairs as you were coming up. As you came to the head of the stairs on the second floor."

"The bedroom of the accused was off the kitchen on the first floor."

"He said his wife slept upstairs and only on several occasions when it was very cold she came down and slept with him."

"During the last three or four weeks due to my wife's nagging I could not sleep and stayed awake half the night, oftentimes hearing two or three o'clock striking, and during the day could not do my work in the woods and hated to come home for dinner?"

"Did he explain why?"

"Because of his wife's quarreling."

Question: "Finally on Saturday, February 2nd, 1957, after her nagging me during the night of February 1st and keeping me awake with her screaming, cursing, shouting and swearing from the time I went to bed about eleven p.m., until one o'clock when she went to bed, the argument was so bad first thing in the morning just after she got up and before she had breakfast, that at about eight a.m. while she was standing on the kitchen floor she called me a whore's bastard."

Question: "Did he tell you why she was nagging that time?"

Answer: "Yes, I think he had been at an AA meeting or was going to it and they were having an argument over the fact he had gone without her – she was tormenting him because he would not take her with him."

Q: "Did he say anything about going to a concert in Baddeck as the reason for her nagging?"

A: "There was some function that he had been to or was going to. I believe a Scottish concert and she had not been asked to go along."

Q: "Did he mention Alex MacLean as having invited him?"

A: "I don't recall."

Q: "Did he disclose to you what he meant by "keeping me awake by her screaming?"

A: "He said he had gone to bed at eleven and his wife had chewed [sic] and had kept yelling at him until around one in the morning." (P 180 CT)

Q: "She called me a 'whore's bastard' and I pushed her and she lost her balance ad fell against the corner of the couch striking her chest on the corner of the couch and knocking herself out...I lost my presence of mind"?
What did he mean by "I lost my presence of mind"?
A: I inferred he could not stand to see anyone suffering and his wife had been suffering after the fall when she cut her head.
Q: What did he mean by "I lost my presence of mind?
Q: He used the term "lost my presence of mind" and also "things went black."
Q: What does it mean?
A: That was his phrase. Then he went upstairs and got the rope.
Q: Did he also say he had been "out of his head?"
A: "I inferred that"
Q: "After you received this statement, C/2, the accused was taken to Baddeck and charged?"
A: "Yes."
Q: "Did you ever try to obtain a third statement?"
A: "No, I never did."

Further detailed questioning of RCMP Officers who had investigated the case completed the trial which was adjourned until May 31, 1957 at 10:00 a.m. On May 31 the prosecutor J. Fisher Hudson and the accused's lawyer Donald MacNeil addressed the Jury for the last time.
There are no transcripts of their presentations.

The actual trial of Dan Murdock Morrison was held May 28, 29, 30, and June 1, 1957. May 31 was lawyer summation to Jury.

JUDGE'S CHARGE TO JURY

On June 1 the presiding judge Hon. Mr. Justice Currie gave his Charge to the Jury.

Judge Currie told the Jury that "all the evidence in this case are circumstantial." No one saw the offence actually committed, so the law makes provision of competent evidence. The Crown must prove the accused intended to kill the deceased person. That he was motivated by an intention to wound or kill. Murder involves intent. He then presented a review of the evidence. Judge Currie told the Jury that he had struggled during the past few nights to try to compress the evidence as briefly as possible.

"The first witness, Alexander MacLean, a near neighbour

of the accused, said that a little after one o'clock in the afternoon of February 2nd the accused called him on the phone and asked him to come over to his house as there was something wrong. He went over. The accused met him at the door and said Daisy has hung herself."

Dr. Gyorfi the medical pathologist performed an autopsy and gave us a detailed description of what he found. He found a cut above the left eyebrow which he concluded was caused by a sharp instrument. There was considerable blood about the head. He judged that after receiving the blow the body had been in a horizontal position or that the head was tipped backwards. He found the tongue protruding, swollen and bitten, and he concluded it was the rope around the neck that caused the tongue to protrude.

He found seven ribs fractured on the left side and seven on the right side. Because the break in each rib was one above the other he concluded that all the ribs had been fractured at the same time and from the same cause. It was his opinion that the deceased woman fell against a hard object which pushed in the chest wall and broke the ribs at the same time. He explained that in a person of her age (about 60) the bones are more brittle that those of a younger person and are liable to fracture more easily. He was definitely of the opinion that the injuries to the ribs did not cause her death.

In the abdomen he found extensive hemorrhage due to a ruptured blood vessel. From the amount of blood found in the abdomen he judged that the blood vessel had oozed blood for about half an hour. He formed the opinion that the ruptured blood vessel was the result of external violence; and that it was not caused by or connected in any way with the rope around the woman's neck.

In his opinion the injury to the stomach area was caused about half and hour before death.

He found swelling of the legs and said it was possible that gravity could have drawn the blood downwards from the ruptured blood vessel in the abdomen.

He found injuries to the shoulders which he said in his opinion were caused by impact with a hard object.

He also told us about the condition of the heart, lungs, kidney and other parts of the body. In his opinion there was nothing in these organs that would cause death.

The most important part of the doctor's evidence is the condition of the neck, internal and external and his conclusions upon the same. In his opinion death was caused by asphyxiation – lack of oxygen in the body – due to constriction of the neck by the rope. The constriction of the neck caused the swollen tongue which stopped the flow of air in the respiratory passage and this produced asphyxiation – the choking to death.

This, he said was consistent with hanging. He said he must believe that these injuries were caused shortly before the hanging – that the deceased woman was definitely alive at the time of hanging.

This was proved by the nature of the constriction marks and other conditions.

The evidence of Sgt. Finney of the R.C.M.P is of the highest importance.
Some question has been raised by the defense about the fact that the accused was in the County jail on the night of February 3rd. You have heard the evidence about that from Sgt. Finney; you have observed his demeanor on the witness stand. You will make up your mind whether or not you believe him. I have no hesitation about it. I believe him, but the matter is for you...
The Judge then said a few words about the high quality of Police and the need for a professional force in society to maintain law and order. (Page 12 of Judge's instructions.) He continued with the trial instructions reviewing for the Jury the evidence given by the police during trial.

(Page 14)

Sgt. Finney said he arrived at the accused's home about 7 p.m. February 2nd, and assisted in the investigation. When it came to be about 8:30 o'clock and became dark, he decided to return to Baddeck. He was not sure whether or not he first suggested to the accused that he come in to Baddeck, but he was sure that at no time did he convey the idea to the accused that he should come to Baddeck. They drove in to the R.C.M.P. detachment, and there was some talk about a night's lodging for him. The accused agreed. They came to the jail and the jailer agreed to keep him for the night. Sgt Finney did not request the jailer to take the accused in, and he said it was possible for the accused to have left the jail if he wanted to.

The next day, the autopsy was performed and that changed the whole picture and changed the view which Finney had about the truth of the statement, C/1, given by the accused to Cpl. Duff. Sgt. Finney then made up his mind that C/1 was not true.

About 1 p.m. of February 3rd he went to the jail, along with Corpl Duff and asked the accused to accompany him to his home. The accused agreed. They were joined by Const. Brook and Tiller

Further investigation of the house and premises was made.

About 4 o'clock the accused made tea and a lunch and he gave some tea to the officers. During the course of the afternoon there had been scraps of conversation between all of them, and about four p.m. Sgt Finney and Corpl. Duff settled down to endeavor to obtain a further statement from the accused. He was told that the autopsy revealed that his wife had broken ribs and a cut on her forehead, injuries to her shoulder. Sgt. Finney said he wanted to get clarification of these and other points from the accused. There had been no reference to these injuries in statement C/1. The accused insisted for some time that statement C/1 was correct. At last Finney asked the accused if he pushed his wife. The accused replied with words to this effect – you will understand that I am not attempting to give the exact words, but I think I am paraphrasing it with reasonable accuracy. You will take your own recollection of the evidence – "You fellows have treated me pretty good. I will tell you the whole story. Yes I pushed her against the couch." Finney said this couch is a home made affair, not upholstered, and is quite hard. The accused then said, in effect, that the fall against the couch had caused his wife to lose consciousness. He carried her from the kitchen to the hall and sat her on a chair, as he thought she might revive in the cool air. She fell off the chair and hit her head on a telephone insulator. She bled quite a lot. He did not want her to suffer. He went upstairs to the room where there was a rope; cut off a piece with his pocket knife; tied it around her neck and tied the other end to the upper banister after pulling her up, and secured the rope.

Gentlemen, that is the gist of the oral statement to which I referred earlier when dealing with the law on the admissibility of statements and other aspects of the law as to the statements, as having been made by the accused to the officers, shortly before he gave statement C/2. You will recall that I said I had ruled on the oral statement as being admissible in evidence. You will recall also that I said to you that you are the sole judges of the weight to be given to that oral statement.

Judge Currie continued to review for the Jury the trial proceedings since the Jury was not present during questioning of the police officers at the trial within a trial. The various officers were called and examined and cross-examined concerning the manner of acquiring evidence and statements from the accused. He told the Jury that statement C/2 is in the nature of a confession while C/1 is not a confession. And it is a true statement from the Judge's perspective. But he left it up to the Jury to decide.

Judge Currie said that the matter of provocation contained in

C/2, raised by the Defence. What the defence urges is that as a result of a wrongful act or insult the accused did what he did in the heat of sudden passion.

It is Section 203 of the Code which sets forth what Parliament has said about provocation:

Section 203 (2)

What is provocation? A wrongful act or insult that is of such a nature as to be sufficient to deprive an ordinary person of the power of self control is provocation for the purposes of this section if the accused acted upon it on the sudden and before there was time for his passion to cool.

Culpable homicide, which would otherwise be murder, may be reduced to manslaughter if the person who causes death does so in the heat of passion caused by sudden provocation.

Provocation is any wrongful act of insult, of such a nature as to be sufficient to deprive an ordinary person of the power of self-control, may be provocation if the offender acts upon it on the sudden, and before there has been time for his passion to cool……

(Page 22 – judge instructions)

The facts in support of the argument on provocation are drawn from statement C/2. …that discloses that the married life of the couple was not happy and that at times the accused felt that it was a hell on earth/ About three or four weeks before her death he could not sleep, sometimes until 2 or 3 o'clock in the morning, because of his wife's nagging. There were times when he hated to come home to his meals. On the night of February 1st she kept him awake with her screaming, shouting, and cursing and swearing until she went to bed about 1 a.m. Saturday morning. The argument was resumed in the morning just after she got up. At about 8 a.m. as she was standing near the couch she called him a 'whore's bastard." He pushed her and she fell against the couch striking her chest, and was knocked out.

If as a result of the prolonged arguments and bickering, the loss of sleep, the resumption of an argument in the morning, and the description of the accused as a "whore's bastard" Mrs. Morrison had been killed when she struck the corner of the bench I might have had to consider whether all that was a wrongful act or insult which produced a heat of passion – a sudden provocation which resulted in her death. But that is not the situation. There is much more to it than that. I leave out of consideration entirely that question as to whether or not the argument between this married couple was a one-sided argument carried on by the wife only. I confine myself to the matter of "a wrongful act or insult" loss of "the power of self-control", "heat of passion", whether there was time for his passion to cool, in the light of Section 203, and of the facts in C/2, and inference from those facts.

Daisy Morrison did not die as a result of being pushed by the accused after he was called a "whore's bastard." The accused must have thought she was alive, for he picked her up and thought if he put her on the chair in the hall where it was cooler she might revive. Were his passions still aflame at that time? I think they were not. Did his passions have time to cool? I think they had. He was not thinking then of a further act of assault on her. His thought then was not of doing her any further harm, but of doing something to revive her. At this time he had sufficient self control, and control of the process of reasoning to know that his wife was not dead, and to feel that if he put her in the hall she might be revived. He acted on that thought by picking her off the floor in the kitchen and putting her on the chair in the hall. I am aware of the law that there is no requirement that the consequent action of a person provoked, and who has been deprived of the power of self-control, shall be confined by him within any limit regulated according to the extent of provocation, R V Linton. It is not the limit of time I am dealing with, it is with the facts in their relation to Section 203.

The accused's wife fell off the chair onto the floor and cut her head on a telephone insulator. He left her on the floor in a pool of blood until he proceeded to reset the stage, the next step in the affair. Just a few feet away from him was a telephone which would connect him with a doctor, a neighbour, the police, with many people. He did not seek help. He said he left her lying in a pool of blood.

I proceed to the next stage to see if there is any evidence to raise an issue under section 203. There now transpires a series of events that speak for themselves.

The accused said that when he saw his wife lying on the floor suffering he lost his presence of mind. Sgt Finney recalled that the words "presence of mind" was proceeded or followed by words by the accused to the effect that he went out of his mind or went off his head. Cpl. Duff recalled that there were some words to the effect that he could not stand to see anyone suffering and also to the effect that things went black on him and that he went off his head.

This woman was a human being. She was his wife. She was

not a dog or a horse that breaks his leg and should be shot to put him out of his suffering. I think it is fair to say that if an ordinary person sees a human being suffering he tried to do what he can to alleviate it or to obtain help. It is said that the very fact that the accused did what he did in the way he did is evidence that his passion had not time to cool and that he was clearly off his head as a result of provocation by the words 'a whore's bastard'".

What is the evidence from which a proper inference can be drawn as to his state of mind? We do not know how long it was after his wife fell on the floor that he went upstairs. He said he went upstairs to where he knew there was a rope. His thought processes appear to have been normal enough to recall that the rope was upstairs. The rope was not just beside him, ready to hand, where he could grab it on a sudden impulse or while in the throes of passion. He had to go upstairs to get it. Why should he have to go for a rope at all? Why would he go for a rope unless he had first of all taken thought of the use to which he intended to put it. I am satisfied that while he was downstairs he took the time to think and plan what he intended to do with the rope. I am satisfied that at this stage, whatever else was in his mind, it was not being propelled by the operation of passion induced by the quarrelling, and the epithet she used. He cut a piece of rope, brought it downstairs, methodically tied a knot on one end and a slip noose on the other end. Then he picked up his badly injured, unconscious wife from the floor, sat her on a chair, tied the noose around her neck, then using the upstairs banister rail as a lever, hauled his wife off the floor and tied the rope securely in a loop around the banister. As a result of this she was strangled to death.

I do not know what time elapsed from the moment he picked her off the floor in the kitchen until he tied the final knot on the banister rail. I am not greatly concerned about that. He said it was about 8 o'clock when they quarreled, and that about 8:30 when he left for the woods. What I am concerned about is to ascertain if there is any evidence to show if there was any period that his passions were so aflame as a result of provocation as to cause a loss of self-control, and if that continued throughout. The Code speaks about the loss of the power of self control by an ordinary man, that is a reasonable man. The test I apply in this case in order to determine whether homicide which is other-wise murder is reduced to manslaughter by reason of a wrongful act of insult, is whether it was sufficient to deprive this particular accused of his power of self control. Because of the conclusion, I have reached on this issue of provocation as a matter of law I am not called upon to consider here and now the conduct of the accused himself as distinct from the conduct of an ordinary person. It is my decision, as a matter of law – law which you are bound to take from me, that there is not any, not the slightest evidence of a wrongful act or insult which would entitle a jury to consider the degree of provocation. Therefore I withdraw from the jury the issue of manslaughter on the ground of provocation.

(Page 27)
The summation of the case for the Crown has been presented to you by Mr. Hudson and does not require any very extended remarks by me. His first point was how she was killed. Is it possible he thought she was dead and hanged her to make it look like suicide? That is discounted by the fact that he said he saw her suffering – he knew she was alive then. Did he on the spur of the moment take her life? The statement says it was 8 a.m. The words "whore's bastard" were used during a quarrel and he pushed her. He says the words "whore's bastard" used during the quarrel are not of sufficient provocation to cause a man to lose his self control.

Furthermore Mr. Hudson said her back must have been to him. I don't think that is necessarily so. I conceive there is a possibility that she was facing him when he pushed her and she wheeled around and fell hitting her chest on the couch. I don't think it necessarily follows that she had her back to him. He urged upon you the importance of the fact that he lifted her up and put her in the hall and it was then after he saw her there that he probably realized what was likely to happen and he then very coolly and calmly determined upon the killing. It was calculated, not sudden, but a deliberate and thought out plan. He saw her lying in a pool of blood and at that time he knew she was living.

The theory of the Defence has been well covered. Mr. MacNeil dealt with some marks on the dead woman's neck and that one possible explanation is that the rope had slipped. There was no positive evidence that the rope had actually slipped.

After the taking of the statement and after consultation with the Crown Prosecutor charge of murder was laid.

Trial

May 25 – JUNE 7, 1957
Baddeck Court House

DAN MURDOCH 'Spinney' MORRISON
BADDECK

"Dan and his wife were not getting along well and they had a lot of squabbles – about money" (p122-transcript)

Page 124 – "she had some money from her previous marriage; more than the accused had and she was lending it the Murdock MacKay and also to the accused; she had paid a considerable amount for work around the house and purchased a car and various things; and her having more money than he has kind of put him – well, he wasn't in the driver's seat. She had the money."

Page 177 - " At times he would jump from one place to another," referring to Spinney statement during interview.

Question – Did he explain to you what their arguments were about?

Answer – yes, he stated some of them were over money.

Q – Did he give you any other reasons?

A – Another was that they never went out together, She/ accused him of going and not taking her."

Page 180 - "Why was she nagging at him? Feb 2? He had gone to an AA meeting or was going to it and they were having an argument over the fact that he had gone without her- she was tormenting him because he would not take her."

MORRISON IS GUILTY OF MURDER
Cape Breton Post, 1957

"Daniel Murdock Morrison, 65, Friday was convicted of the rope-slaying of his wife Daisy, 62, by Supreme Court petit jury which deliberated 75 minutes.

SHOWS NO EMOTION

The stocky, almost-bald carpenter and woodsman, scratched his head, stopped chewing on the ever-present peppermints, but showed no emotion as petit jury foreman Leonard Harvey, a Baddeck Surveyor, answered "guilty" in a low tone voice to the question of Cape Breton County Prothonotary A.D Muggah, "How say you, guilty, or not guilty?"

The courtroom was hushed, tense. There was hardly a stir as the verdict was read.

Then Mr. Justice L.D Currie, obviously worn by the first capital punishment trial in 23 years in Victoria County, said sentence would be pronounced Saturday at 10 a.m.

Under the Canadian Criminal Code sentence by hanging is mandatory.

Defence Counsel Donald MacNeil, MLA, Sydney, said an appeal was likely.

Mr. Justice Currie gave his charge to the jury in one hour and 45 minutes, and in it he withdrew from the jury "the issue of manslaughter on the grounds of provocation."

Appendix D – McEachen Family Tragedy

October 8, 1894
Halifax Evening Mail

Saturday afternoon witnessed the penultimate act of the great McEachen tragedy. The final feature will be the analyst's report and the jury's findings.

McEachen and his wife are laid away forever in a corner of the Dartmouth public cemetery and according to the rites of the Church of England. In the fold of the Episcopal belief they were born and married and died. They repose side by side in a common grave, unmarked as yet except by two mounds of earth above. There are two caskets and there were two hearses. It was a solemn cortege from the house to the burying ground. Alex, age 13, the only son, was among the mourners. His three sisters, one older and two younger, had been brought home to view the remains of their parents before they were borne away. The funeral started at three o'clock. There was a large number in attendance. At the grave side the son cried as though his heart would break. Nobody could comfort the child. All four children are with their uncle now. The furniture of their desolate home was removed to-day. It was tendered the landlady, Mrs. Wright, in payment of five months in arrears of rent but she charitably refused to receive it. Mrs. Wright let the orphaned children have the few things. The house is empty. It is a very old building, one of the oldest in Dartmouth. There are many things about the premises that suggest the inner life of the McEachen family during their residence there since May. For instance the yard is grown with weeds and bestrewn with debris, a creeper climbing on the shingles needs trimming badly and there is a pile of shore wood that was gathered for fuel. Yesterday forenoon a stranger attracted to the place by curiosity, found a pair of pet rabbits in a wicker box in the coal shed. They had been forgotten since Thursday and were quite fierce. Speaking of this incident afterward to a neighbour, the latter remarked that the McEachens had been very distant.

Throughout the five months they occupied Mrs. Wright's, few visitors called and few visits were paid. Mrs. McEachen was never seen out of doors and Maud, the eldest daughter, rarely. Mr. McEachen was seen so little that it was thought that he went away each morning to Halifax to work. Once only he exchanged a word with a passer by. The boy played with other boys for a week or so and then left them and sought older companions. He was too grave and reticent to take part in their joyous games. The lad went to school. The two little girls made acquaintance with neighbours' daughters of their own age, but never talked much about themselves or their home. The McEachen children were always dressed neatly.   They concealed their indigence as effectively as the older members of the family. It is doubtful if a single soul outside the McEachens themselves suspected how hard life had been with them for five months.

There is no doubt that hardship and vicissitude were the cause of the three deaths. Three deaths there certainly were – not two. It was a triple, not a double, tragedy.

Regarding the death of Mrs. McEachen, there is additional proof that that melancholy event took place Thursday evening, as reported by the MAIL, and not Friday morning. The further testimony on this head is independent of a reiterated statement of Dr. Cunningham's to the same effect. The doctor declares again positively that when he saw the body of the woman 8:30 Friday morning rigor mortis in his opinion had set in, and that death had taken place at least twelve hours previous.

Of course he did not make a critical examination. That was not necessary, the rigidity of the limbs being apparent.

The additional evidence is the sense of smell of several persons who arrived at the house early after Dr. Cunningham. They remarked the odor of decomposition being very strong in the house. That could hardly be if Mrs. McEachen had died only a couple of hours before, as Doctors Smith and Jacques claim.

It seems as though it will never be known whether Mrs. McEachen took poison, deliberately or by administration of which she was unaware. The uncertainty as to the hour of her demise throws an uncertainty over all conjectures. The analysis may or may not reveal poison in her stomach. It will be no surprise if it does not. Of course there is the husband's note saying his wife had been poisoned, which creates a belief that she was. If a combination of cyanogens was used, it may have left no trace, as many of these do, being volatile.

Another mysterious thing is the absence of any poison remaining in the house of the kind that it is thought was used. The way the doctors conclude a deadly poison was the agent is because of the rapidity that death was produced in the case of the man. At 5:30 o'clock, and at a time a little later he wrote notes in a clear bold hand and was left by his daughter as in good health, and two hours afterward he was found dead.

But search high and low has failed to find any such poison about the premises, or a bottle or box that might have contained such poison. There are two channels of explanation. One, that some person took the bottle away after McEachen was dead, and the other that he threw it in the stove. A fire was started in the kitchen stove through the day which obliterated any clue that might have been there. The fire was started before anybody thought of looking in the stove.

Friday, October 5, 1894
Halifax Evening Mail
A Tragic Affair In Dartmouth
Man and Wife found dead this morning.
Was It Murder Or Suicide?

Alexander McEachen, formerly Sexton of the First Baptist Church and Mrs. McEachen the victims. She was dead in her bed and he was lifeless in the kitchen. Poison found in the house. A Note from the Husband Says His Wife was accidentally poisoned. The Inquest to be held this evening.

Across the harbor in Dartmouth, two hundred yards north of the ferry on Water Street, is a house that might fittingly be termed a chamber of horrors. It is an old pitch roof cottage, sandwiched in between the tall new residence of John T. Walker, contractor, on the south side, and another house the same size as the fateful one on the north. Within the building Alexander McEachen and Alice McEachen, his wife, are both dead, poisoned.

Their lifeless bodies were found this morning about 8 o'clock by the children, the eldest child, aged 15, ran away for Dr. Cunningham, who returned with the girl and found father and mother dead beyond all recall. Mrs. McEachen was lying on her right side in the bed and her husband reposed in the basement kitchen in the same manner. The woman's head drooped on the pillow. The bed clothes were rolled down from her neck and shoulders and the left arm was outside the counterpane. Mr. McEachen had pants, socks and woolen shirt on. His feet were toward the kitchen door, which was open, and which opens into the hall running from the backyard to the street wall. The stairs terminate on the side of this hall opposite the kitchen door.

The dead man's head was from the door. His face was turned toward the window which looks out on the harbor and the city (Halifax) over the way. The shore is only forty feet from the building. The railroad track passes between. There is an entrance from that quarter.

After leaving the track and traversing the yard, the yard door communicates with the hall referred to. From the yard door to the kitchen door is four feet perhaps. On a plain deal table near Mr. McEachen's body stood a glass goblet and beside it an oblong piece of white unruled paper, Written upon it with blue pencil in a clear bold hand was the laconic message:

wife accidentally poisoned.
i cannot stand the loss go to join her.

Capitals were omitted from the note. The piece of paper was about 6 ½ inches long by 2 ¾ wide. The goblet was not placed over the note to keep it down nor was there any paper weight.

A small quantity of liquid remained in the goblet. Dr. Cunningham detected a hydrocyanic odor and thought the liquid was prussic acid. W.A. Dymond, druggist, was handed the fatal glass. He thought it had contained a caustic poison and did not agree with Dr. Cunningham. Coroner Weeks' nostrils did not catch the odor of a cyanide either. The kitchen store had no fire in it; an overcast fall sky appeared outside. Rain drops fell down past the window panes from the cap of the sash and the apartment was as cheerless as it possibly could be. The face of the prostrate man was bloated somewhat. The eyes were half closed, arms and legs were not rigid. The body rolled over on its back after awhile. A more ghastly hue stole over the countenance and colour fled from the hands and bare wrists. A white cloth was charitably spread over the body by the constable until a jury was summoned.

The staircase ascending to the first floor proper is a dark, old-fashioned, boxed-in affair. It is winding and narrow. It enters the upper hall, running from the street door to the rear of the house, nearly opposite the door of the bed room where mrs. M'eachen was found. This room is at the back of the flat. It is ten feet square, or a little better. There is communication through a closet to the front room, and latterly to a little room, where the four children slept. This little room is the hall extension. The hall does not run to the rear wall of the house. Access to the children's apartment in through the mother's chamber. The four children are Maud, 15, Alec, 13, Daisy, 10, Minnie, 8. A five months' old child died. All four occupied one large bed. Daisey attends Miss Scarfe's grade at Park school. Minnie's teacher is Miss Pender. They were both at school yesterday. Maud has not been to school since her father moved from Halifax. In the city she attended Morris street school. The children are remarkably bright and apt. The flow of language, elegance of diction and self-possession of the eldest daughter is unaccountable. Father and mother had an ordinary common school education. There are not a dozen books in the house. The same ready address is a possession of the boy and his two younger sisters.

The little ones were weeping bitterly today but between their tears answered all questions freely and concisely. Persons who were attracted to the afflicted household wondered as they listened.

Maud McEachen, the eldest daughter, was met by an evening mail reporter in the hall way. This was an hour after Dr. Cunningham's first visit. There is a porch projecting upon Water Street. The inner door was locked by a spring bolt. The young girl withdrew that and admitted the reporter in response to a knock.

"Who are you?" she asked Being told she said she knew not what to do but would like if no investigation were undertaken until her uncle, Harvey Saville, foreman at the Ordnance, arrived. He had been sent for in haste. The girl was soothing the youngest children. They were sobbing aloud.

Daisy, one of these, told what she knew.

"Minnie and I were in bed this morning. Father came in about six o'clock and said he had sent Maud and Alec over for our uncle. He said mamma was better this morning. He went down stairs. Later we heard a noise like a fall in the kitchen. I asked Minnie what was that bang. She said it was the door closing. It must have been father falling off the chair. We saw mamma afterward and

She was not breathing. When people don't breathe they are dead."

Renewed sobbing interrupted the child's statement for a moment. Then she went on.

"Yesterday mamma fell down in a faint. She was in bed all day. We went to school. Father said we were in the way. When he came in this morning he said mamma was better. When we found father down stairs this morning while Maud and Alec were over in Halifax, we thought he was sleeping. He used to lay his head on the table and go to sleep and we thought he had rolled off. Minnie said he was dead. We asked Maud when she came back and she said father was sleeping."

Maud said, "father and mother both belong to Woolwich, England. They were married there. Mother was a couple of months older than father. He loved her dearly always. He worked in the Imperial Arsenal there one time. He was never in the army. I was born at Woolwich. Alec , Daisy and Minnie were born in Brooklyn, N. Y. to which city father moved fourteen years ago (1880). We lived there seven years (until 1887). I was too young to know what father worked at there or what was the number of his house and name of the street. I know he worked on Coney Island.

We came to halifax seven years ago (1887/1888) and lived for a long while at the North West Arm. For three years prior to May last (1894) father was sexton of the First Baptist Church (Queen Street at Spring Garden Road intersection, Halifax, Nova Scotia) and we lived over the vestry. He worked in the daytime for the Imperial Government on St. George's Island. At first he returned home at four o'clock in the afternoon and then attended to his duties in connection with church. A new officer took charge at the government works and made father work later. So he left the government employ, and depended for three or four weeks on the sexton's salary. He could not find a job that he could get, and at the same time attend to the church.

(He had a government job, why did he not stay with it? His first love was photography and he had time to do it with the Church work maybe; whereas the government job was full time. Also housing was very expensive in Halifax at that time; a lot of military activity, prostitution, shipping).

Uncle Harvey advised him to go to Dartmouth. He would get a cheap house there. He resigned from the church in May (1894) and moved to Dartmouth. He tried several places before getting this house. Shortly after coming over here he was seized with inflammatory rheumatism and had been unable to do anything since.

(Was he ill before this move? Was the illness caused by photographic chemicals or stresses of having to raise a family in Halifax where British government jobs were plentiful, but good housing expensive?)

Yesterday morning mother fainted (Thursday, October 4, 1894). She reposed in a semi-unconscious state all day and last night. This morning father sent Alec and I over to uncle's in the ?? ferry??(unreadable) boat. Mother was alive then. She was breathing. I did not see her but father said she was breathing easier. Alec and I went to uncle's. He lives in the Ordnance. He read the note from father, but said he could not come just then as work was pressing. We got back about eight o'clock and found everything as you see it. I instantly sent Alec back to uncle's for the children's sake.

I dare not give way to my feelings. I do not know what made father do it. Mother was dead in her room when I got back, the children were frightened, the goblet and note were on the table in the kitchen and father was dead on the floor. I told the children he was sleeping.

There had been no medicines obtained for the house for some time. I always bought the groceries. At Mr. Dymonds a month ago I bought five cents worth of laudanum. That is in the bureau half unused. That was for father's rheumatism. It was applied externally. I do not know where the liquid that was in the goblet came from. Father was not out yesterday. He went to bed shortly after ten o'clock last night. He sent Alec over to Jas. Scott & Co's for some brandy for mother. Mother has been sick off and on for a long while. She was to have washed the family's linen today. The only thing she drank yesterday was a glass of the brandy. She fainted then. About eleven o'clock in the morning she regained consciousness and said to Daisy,

"Be good." She did not speak to Minnie or me.

She never spoke again to my knowledge."

Harvey Saville and wife (Clara) arrived at the house about 9:30 o'clock this morning. He is the brother of the dead woman. Mr. Saville's mother and two other sisters of his are in San Francisco, California. These are the only relatives in America. Mr. Saville was shocked and amazed. He received his brother-in-law's note before he was out of bed this morning. It was brief and written in blue lead pencil. It ran come quickly something serious.

That was all. He thought it was just an ordinary case where some substantial assistance was required. He had helped his brother-in-law several times through the summer. Maud told him about her mother being sick and said she was better when she left. Mr. Saville concluded the case was not preemptory and as he had urgent work to perform this morning he set about doing that before complying with the request of his brother-in-law. The next he learned was from Alec, who returned from Dartmouth with a message from Maud that both the father and mother were dead. Mr. Saville says he never had reason to believe his brother-in-law would commit suicide. He was an amateur photographer when a young man and was quite proficient at it.

He knew McEachen understood the uses of the various acids.

It will be noted that when McEachen gave his daughter the note in Halifax that he wrote come quickly, something serious. And at the same time informed the children their mother was better. Not one of the children actually saw the mother early. McEachen had been by his wife all night. The hour the two children heard the heavy fall was just after the departure of the other two for Halifax. McEachen went down stairs immediately after dispatching the message to his brother-in-law. ... (unreadable few words) One theory is that Mrs. McEachen died during that period. Maud says she did not exchange a word with her mother since Wednesday. Arriving home from the city yesterday afternoon she passed her mother's bed. Mrs. McEachen was then motionless. Her face was turned away and could not be seen. The girl did not approach to ascertain if her mother was breathing. The father said his wife was all right. She lay still yesterday afternoon, last night and this morning. All this time the woman was undoubtedly dead. The father managed to deceive the children. Coming daylight today, after drinking the brandy, and after a night in company with the inanimate body of his wife and fearful of what the day would bring, investigation, apprehension, etc., it is supposed he at last nerved himself for the final coup and ended his own life. McEachen was a dreamer. For the last four months he had done no work. He tried hard to get work. He asked assistance from many sources. The visit of his oldest daughter to Halifax yesterday was to procure a loan of money from a friend. The family was in want of food. They had good clothes but very little to eat. A few pieces of bread were all that the officers found in the shape of food to-day.

The inquest

Coroner W. H. Weeks empanelled a jury soon after the news of the tragedy became public. Edward Graham as foreman. The jurors viewed the bodies and the premises, ordered a post mortem examination and adjourned to meet again at seven 0'clock this evening. Dr. M.A. B. Smith had Dr. H.S. Jacques associated with him performing the post mortem and analysis of the content of the stomachs, the goblet and several medicine bottles found in the house. These physicians will give their testimony to night.

In the meantime the dwelling of the McEachen's is locked up. Chief of Police McKenzie and Officer Brennan have it under surveillance. The bodies are just where they were found. Very little has been disturbed. Drawers and cupboards were ransacked for bottles and papers by the police acting under authority. Searching the house was not an extensive job. There are several large trunks unpacked in the chief bedroom. The attic rooms are unoccupied. The front room on the street contains bric-a-brac and a couple of articles of furniture. A stove is conspicuous for its dark fireless bars. The floor is bare.

The bedrooms are uncarpeted also. There are cheap blinds on the windows. The kitchen dresser downstairs is well stocked with crockery ware. There is not much else in the building. The orphaned children are with friends or neighbours. Mrs. Saville, wife of Fore-

man Saville of the Ordnance stated that in England McEachen and his wife were temporarily separated or in trouble of some kind. He wrote her a letter saying his dead body would probably be found in the river Thames if something did not turn up. Among McEachen's papers were the couple's marriage lines. The certificate reads thus:
Marriage solemnized at the parish church in the parish of Woolwich, in the county of Kent.

No. 86, seventeenth June, 1878, Charles Alexander McEachen, bachelor, photographer, 10 James Place, son of John McEachen, blacksmith, and Alice Saville, spinster, daughter of Matthew Saville, cabinet maker. Married in the parish church according to the rites of the established church after bans by me, E.C. Robinson. In the presence of Matthew Saville and Caroline Saville. I certify that the above is a true copy, dated the 17th day of June, 1878. E.C. Robinson, Assistant Curate.

Findings

Inquisition in to Demise Alice Mary Ann McEachen and Alexander Charles McEachen - October 5th 1894.

Maude McEachen being sworn saith "I am daughter of Alice Mary Ann McEachen and Alexander McEachen – of whose bodies the jury have now viewed. My mother had been ill about four months. About half past five o'clock this morning my father waked me and said that I should go over to Halifax and ask my uncle Matthew Saville to come over. I went over. My uncle said he could not possibly come then but would do his best to come over. I caught the six o' clock ferry back. On my return I found my father laying on the kitchen floor in the same position that the jury saw him. I went upstairs and found my mother in the same position she is in now. I sent right away for Dr. Cunningham. Father has been out of work ever since he has been here that is since last May." Witness identified her father's hand writing on a paper handed in by Policeman Brennin, it read thus "wife accidentally poisoned I cannot stand the loss. I go to join her." "My father used to do photography in England never did any in this country at home, but has taken pictures outside some pictures with Captain Ross in about five or six years ago. Night before last my mother took some supper. Yesterday morning when I went to her room she was sleeping and breathing heavily, about 8 o' clock she tried to get up and fell back father went to get her a little brandy but she fell back and he did not give it to her. I saw her several times during the day she was always sleeping. I was in my mother's room this morning just before leaving for Halifax my mother was breathing then and my father seemed all right." A bottle was produced by Policeman Brennin which witness identified as one said to contain brandy – "the bottle was half full yesterday. This morning it was empty – I saw my father take some right from this bottle, I mean he drank it."

Signed Maud McEachen.

The jury unanimously requested a post mortem examination of the bodies. And the coroner adjourned the inquest until seven o'clock for that purpose.

Inquisition resumed at seven o'clock.

Montaque A. B. Smith being sworn saith – "I am a Physician and in practice in Dartmouth; I was called upon by the coroner to hold a post-mortem examination on the bodies of Alice McEachen and Alexander C. McEachen. At 3:45 this afternoon I commenced the post mortem of the body of Alexander McEachen – assisted by Dr. H.S. Jacques of Halifax. I found the body laying on its back on the floor of the kitchen – arms extended one leg extended , the slightly flexed – right side of the face eschemised[7]. This would indicate that the deceased had lain on his right side some time after death.

The ecchymoses was of a peculiar mottled character different from what occurs after death from natural causes. Eyes closed pupils normal. Clothing consisting of shirt – undershirt pants drawers and socks. No marks of violence on body. On opening the abdomen no peculiar odor was noticeable. The stomach was considerably congested describable by transmitted light. The stomach was secured but not opened. The lungs appeared to be slightly congested and somewhat engorged with dark venous blood. The blood that escaped on making incisions was darker than usually found after death, Heart healthy, kidneys also. The intestines were congested in spots. I did not examine the brain, none of these conditions are sufficient to indicate the cause of death. The lungs appear normal spleen slightly congested – I would conclude from all the facts that Alexander McEachen must have come to his death from either external violence or poison – from the indications I would not look for apoplexy though it might possibly be the cause of death – I preserved the stomach because I was not satisfied as to the cause of death and with the anticipation that the jury might order the contents of the stomach to be analyzed. I also preserved a

---

7   ecchymosis pl. ecchymoses A bluish discolouration of an area of skin or mucous membrane caused by the extravasation of blood into the subcutaneous tissues as a result of trauma to the underlying blood vessels or fragility of the vessel walls.(Mosby's Medical Dictionary, 8th edition. © 2009, Elsevier.)

small quantity of a white liquid which I found in a wine glass. I have it in a small sealed bottle.

I then proceeded to make a post-mortem on the body of Alice McEachen. I found the lady lying in an easy position across the bed on the right side – clothing consisted of night dress – bed clothes did not indicate any struggle – legs extended – right arm extended, left forearm lying across the chest, large amount of blood stained ----- froth oozing from nostrils – hands tightly clutched. Right side of the body ecchymosed, face mottled and eccemosed, pupils somewhat dilated, goose flesh appearance of skin, hands very much eccemosed. On opening abdomen no peculiar odor detected; Deceased was pregnant about six or seven months. Heart, lungs, spleen, liver, kidneys generally healthy with the exception of a general congestion of the viscous system. The stomach was secured and removed and preserved.

It showed congestion also. From the post-mortem examination and other ……..? I have been so far unable to form any definite opinion as to the causes of death – Rigor mortis had not set in at 5:30 when we commenced the post-mortem on her body – but had already set in on the body of the man-in answer to the foreman of the jury- In the case of the woman rigor mortis may have set in and passed away in the intervention of decomposition – which would not be likely to occur for several days. With the Chief of Police I found a box labeled 'Rough on Rats'. The box was half-full of a grayish colour powder. It is my opinion that in order to come to any positive conclusion as to the cause of death in either case an analysis of the contents of the stomach should be made.

—Montague A. B. Smith MD

Hartley S. Jacques being sworn saith "I am a Physician and practice in Halifax. I was requested by Dr. M. A. B. Smith the last witness to assist him in making an autopsy on the bodies of Alice Mary Ann McEachen and Alexander McEachen laying dead at Dartmouth. I have heard the evidence of the Court Witness Dr. M.A.B. Smith and I concur with him in so far as his statements as to this autopsy is concerned. I found on the body of Alexander McEachen nothing to justify me to form an opinion as to the cause of death. I am of opinion that for this investigation such as chemical analysis of the contents of the stomach or materials found about the house might throw further light as to the cause of death.

—H.S. Jacques M.D.

The Coroner put the question to the jury "Do you consider a chemical examination of the contents of the stomach advisable and do you request the same?" The jury retired to consider the matter and shortly returned and demanded chemical analyses of the contents of the stomach in both cases.

Thereupon the coroner adjourned the inquest to Friday 2th instant to be resumed at the Town Hall Dartmouth at 7 o'clock evening.

Inquisition Resumed at the Town Hall Dartmouth, Friday 12 October 1894 -

Daniel Brennan being sworn saith "I am a police constable and live in Dartmouth. I am acting as coroner constable on this inquest. On Friday the fifth of October I was called to deceased house by telephone by Dr. Cunningham. I found the bodies pretty much in the position described by former witnesses.

October 8, 1894
Halifax Evening Mail

THERE WERE THREE DEATHS NOT TWO

Additional Proof that Mrs. McEachen had been Dead for Hours Before the Discovery – Particulars of the Burial Saturday – Mystery about the Poison that Did the Work

Saturday afternoon witnessed the penultimate act of the great McEachen tragedy. The final feature will be the analyst's report and the jury's findings.

McEachen and his wife are laid away forever in a corner of the Dartmouth public cemetery and according to the rites of the Church of England. In the fold of the Episcopal belief they were born and married and died. They repose side by side in a common grave, unmarked as yet except by two mounds of earth above. There are two caskets and there were two hearses. It was a solemn cortege from the house to the burying ground. Alex, age 13, the only son, was among the mourners. His three sisters, one older and two younger, had been brought home to view the remains of their parents before they were borne away.

The funeral started at three o'clock. There was a large number in attendance. At the grave side the son cried as though his heart would break. Nobody could comfort the child. All four children are with their uncle now. The furniture of their desolate home was removed to-day. It was tendered the landlady, Mrs. Wright, in payment of five months in arrears of rent but she charitably refused to receive it. Mrs. Wright let the orphaned children have the few things. The house is empty. It is a very old building, one of the oldest in Dartmouth. There are many things about the premises that suggest the inner life of the McEachen family during their residence there since May. For instance the yard is grown with weeds and bestrewn with debris, a creeper climbing on the shingles needs trimming badly and there is a pile of shore wood that was gathered for fuel. Yesterday forenoon a stranger attracted to the place by curiosity, found a pair of pet rabbits in a wicker box in the coal shed. They had been forgotten since Thursday and were quite fierce. Speaking of this incident afterward to a neighbour, the latter remarked that the McEachen's had been very distant. Throughout the five months they occupied Mrs. Wright's, few visitors called and few visits were paid. Mrs. McEachen was never seen out of doors and Maud, the eldest daughter, rarely. Mr. McEachen was seen so little that it was thought that he went away each morning to Halifax to work. Once only he exchanged a word with a passer by. The boy played with other boys for a week or so and then left them and sought older companions. He was too grave and reticent to take part in their joyous games. The lad went to school. The two little girls made acquaintance with neighbours' daughters of their own age, but never talked much about themselves or their home. The McEachen children were always dressed neatly. They concealed their indigence as effectively as the older members of the family. It is doubtful if a single soul outside the McEachens themselves suspected how hard life had been with them for five months. There is no doubt that hardship and vicissitude were the cause of the three deaths. Three deaths there certainly were – not two. It was a triple, not a double, tragedy.

Regarding the death of Mrs. McEachen there is additional proof that that melancholy event took place Thursday evening, as reported by the MAIL, and not Friday morning. The further testimony on this head is independent of a reiterated statement of Dr. Cunningham's to the same effect. The doctor declares again positively that when he saw the body of the woman 8:30 Friday morning rigor mortis in his opinion had set in, and that death had taken place at least twelve hours previous.

Of course he did not make a critical examination. That was not necessary, the rigidity of the limbs being apparent.

The additional evidence is the sense of smell of several persons who arrived at the house early after Dr. Cunningham. They remarked the odor of decomposition being very strong in the house. That could hardly be if Mrs. McEachen had died only a couple of hours before, as Doctors Smith and Jacques claim. It seems as though it will never be known whether Mrs. McEachen took poison, deliberately or by administration of which she was unaware. The uncertainty as to the hour of her demise throws an uncertainty over all conjectures. The analysis may or may not reveal poison in her stomach. It will be no surprise if it does not. Of course there is the husband's note saying his wife had been poisoned, which creates a belief that she was. If a combination of cyanigen was used, it may have left no trace, as many of these do, being volatile.

Another mysterious thing is the absence of any poison remaining in the house of the kind that it is thought was used. The way the doctors conclude a deadly poison was the agent is because of the rapidity that death was produced in the case of the man. At 5:30 o'clock, and at a time a little later he wrote notes in a clear bold hand and was left by his daughter as in good health, and two hours afterward he was found dead.

But search high and low has failed to find any such poison about the premises, or a bottle or box that might have contained such poison. There are two channels of explanation. One, that some person took the bottle away after McEachen was dead, and the other that he threw it in the stove. A fire was started in the kitchen stove through the day which obliterated and clue that might have been there. The fire was started before anybody thought of looking in the stove.

"I do not know what made Father Do It" (Maud McEachen October 5, 1894)

"One of my cousins said there was a skeleton in the cupboard.[8]"

Author's Note:

Charles Alexander and Alice McEachen died from cyanide poisoning on October 5, 1894. From appearances at the time it was believed that abject poverty and unemployment were the causes of Alec's despondency. They were reduced to begging from family, borrowing from shop keepers, selling their few possessions to provide food. Alec's father died in Woolwich in 1890 which added to his despair being unable to afford travel to England to comfort his mother. Possibly his father was sending money to help with expenses. Alexander administered cyanide to his wife and then to himself. Leaving the four children with neither father nor mother.

However, a newspaper report on October 8, 1894 headline read

---

[8] Trudy Baker, August 16, 2012 from England, a distant relative of Alice.

"There were three deaths not two" opens the door to another reason for the deaths.

When Alice and Alec moved to Dartmouth in May 1894, Alice was two months pregnant with their fifth child. Potassium cyanide had been for many years used to cause miscarriages and abortions. Cyanide was sold openly in grocery stores, drug stores and freely and easily available. It had been used in photography for developing pictures and hundreds of photographers and their family members died from accidental ingestion.

Under pressure and despair, Alec and Alice decided they could not financially handle another child. Alec knew how to administer the tincture of potassium to solve their problem. However, he probably made a mistake and Alice was affected by the poison. She lingered for months getting weaker and weaker. There was no free medical care at the time. No government paid care, no welfare, no child support programs. People were on their own except for some religious societies that tried to help the needy.

The failed abortion attempt put the fear of the Law into Alec. Not only was he unemployed, sickly, broke but after he and Alice tried to abort her pregnancy, they were now criminals according to Canadian Law.

Abortion Law in Canada[9]

In 1892, the federal Canadian Criminal Code made every aspect of abortion illegal. It was illegal to discuss, find materials for, or perform abortions. Nearly the same was true for contraception. A slight leniency allowed abortion when it would save the life of the pregnant woman, and the most severe penalty - life imprisonment - was reserved for practitioners of the procedure.

It was also against the law for a woman to seek an abortion, to allow one to be performed on herself, or to self-abort, but, by the mid-20th century, women who were found out, usually because they were rushed to hospital bleeding or poisoned, were often not subjected to legal punishment. That did not prevent the police from questioning a frightened, bed-ridden hospital patient; the police often hounded women who had had abortions, demanding information about who had performed the procedure.

While Alice was dying from the accidental poisoning, Alec was in a difficult place. He could not afford a doctor. He had no money to buy antidote to cyanide poisoning. When Alice died and found to have been pregnant, he would go to prison for life.

Under the Criminal Code of Canada passed by Parliament in 1892,

---

9　　http://umanitoba.ca/colleges/st_pauls/ccha/Back%20Issues/CCHA1986/Beahan.pdf

there were two ways in which a person accused of being involved with an abortion could be charged, either for attempting to procure a miscarriage or for supplying a drug or an instrument intended for use to procure a miscarriage. If police failed to produce convincing evidence against a practitioner of this crime, they could charge him or her with the more minor offence of practicing medicine without a licence...For abortion the most serious charge which could be levelled was attempting to procure a miscarriage.

Chapter 23, Section 272 of the Canadian Criminal Code for 1892 made liable for life imprisonment anyone who attempted to procure a miscarriage on a woman through drug or instrument whether she was pregnant or only believed to have been pregnant. Section 273 of the same act made the pregnant woman liable to seven years in prison who herself attempted, or permitted others to attempt to procure an abortion through drugs or instruments whether the woman was pregnant or only believed to have been pregnant[10].

There was only the very small residue in the goblet on the table where Alexander McEachen had been sitting. Alternatively, the police discovered that a well-known widely used rat poison was in the house. 'Rough on Rats' was used extensively in Canada and the USA for suicide. There was disagreement among the doctors and druggist before the inquest as to the actual poison used. Rough on Rats was mostly arsenic[11].

---

10   Canada, Sessional Papers, 1892, "An 8 Act Respecting the Criminal Code,"55-56 V.
11   http://www.trutv.com/library/crime/notorious_murders/women/creighton_applegate/6.html

Appendix E - Obituary of Attorney John MacIvor

John Smith MacIvor[12]

Brief Summary of the
Obituary of John (J.) Smith MacIvor Q.C.
(From Cape Breton Post, Sydney, NS, Thursday June 13, 1957)

"The Honorable John Smith MacIvor was a son of Kate Smith and Malcolm MacIvor who were among the first residents of Glace Bay. His father was representative for Chappells Limited for more than 40 years. Mr. MacIvor graduated from Glace Bay High School after which he entered Acadia University, Wolfville, NS., where he received a B.A. degree and went on to Dalhousie University, Halifax, to graduate in Law in 1937.

"A popular and esteemed figure on the local and Provincial scene, J. Smith MacIvor, Q.C., 44, died Wednesday in the Sydney City Hospital and the news of his passing has occasioned deep grief and sorrow throughout the Maritimes.

Former Speaker of the Nova Scotia Legislature, he was described Wednesday night by Premier Robert L. Stanfield, Q.C., as 'a politician who won the respect and affection of members on all sides of the house.'

His death Wednesday, June 12, ended a period of illness that began 10 years ago. Death was due to rheumatoid arthritis from which he continuously suffered since 1947. He entered Provincial politics in 1945.

---

[12]   Source: http://trees.ancestry.com/tree/14298485/person/87185414

First Practice

North Sydney was the site of his first practice of law. He remained in the Northside town for almost a year when he moved to Sydney and in subsequent years was joined by Allister Ross, Sydney lawyer, and the partnership operated under the name of MacIvor and Ross.

He was admitted to the Bar in 1937 and became Cape Breton Magistrate in 1942. He continued in that capacity until 1945 when he was elected Liberal Member for Cape Breton South (Sydney). Mr. MacIvor continued in the House in the succeeding elections of 1949 and 1953 but was defeated in the October 1956 Election (by PC candidate Barrister Donald C. MacNeil). He became Speaker of the House in 1954, nine years after he was first elected. Following his loss in the 1956 election, he resumed his practice of law. He was a popular and esteemed figure on the local and provincial scene. In April 1957 he became Provincial Magistrate for Cape Breton Island.

Throughout his political and legal tenure, Mr. MacIvor suffered from debilitating rheumatoid arthritis continually from 1947 until his death.

Mr. MacIvor never married."

J. Smith MacIvor Dies In Hospital

(From Cape Breton Post, Sydney, NS, Thursday June 13, 1957)

A popular and esteemed figure on the local and Provincial scene, J. Smith MacIvor, Q.C., 44, died Wednesday in the Sydney City Hospital and the news of his passing has occasioned deep grief and sorrow throughout the Maritimes.

Former Speaker of the Nova Scotia Legislature, he was described Wednesday night by Premier Robert L. Stanfield, Q.C., as "a politician who won the respect and affection of members on all sides of the House."

His death, Wednesday ended a period of illness that began 10 years ago. Death was due to rheumatoid arthritis from which he continuously suffered since 1947. Despite the terrific impact of the painful ailment he continued his daily duties with marked courage, sunny disposition, and a Spartan spirit that won him the admiration of countless citizens, irrespective of political persuasion, the length and breadth of the Province.

He entered Provincial politics in 1945 when he was elected

Liberal member for the riding of Cape Breton South (Sydney) defeating at that time Provincial CCF Leader Donald MacDonald now the Secretary-treasurer of Canada's powerful Canadian Labour Congress. Mr. MacIvor continued in the House in the succeeding elections of 1949 and 1953, but went down to defeat in the October Provincial elections of 1956 when his successor was P.C. candidate Donald MacNeil, well known Sydney barrister.

He became Speaker of the House in 1954, nine years after he was first elected, and his predecessor was Gordon Romkey, Lunenburg, M.L.A.

Mr. MacIvor entered the hospital, Tuesday night, after his illness took on serious and final aspects more than a week ago.

Death came Wednesday morning shortly after nine o'clock when he was suddenly stricken with cardiac arrest and died within minutes before his person physician, Dr. Arthur Ormiston reached the scene.

Tributes

Led by Nova Scotia Premier Robert l. Stanfield, .., prominent citizens Wednesday night paid tribute to the memory of J. Smith MacIvor, Q.C., Lawyer and former Speaker of the Nova Scotia Legislature who died Wednesday in the Sydney City Hospital.

PREMIER STANFIELD

Nova Scotian will learn with regret of the death of j. Smith MacIvor of Sydney. Mr. MacIvor was a friendly, generous man, greatly liked by all with whom he came in contact. He represented the city of Sydney in the legislature from 1945 to 1956.

From 1953 to 1956 Mr. MacIvor was speaker in the House of Assembly. He discharged his difficult responsibilities in a manner that earned him respect and affection of members on all sides of the house.

Final Tribute Paid To Smith MacIvor
(From Cape Breton Post, Sydney, NS, Thursday June 13, 1957)

From the cities, the town, and rural districts throughout the province, hundreds of citizens from all walks of life assembled in Sydney Friday evening to pay final tribute to the memory of a great Nova Scotian – J. Smith MacIvor, Q.C., Lawyer and popular legislator.

Funeral services were held in the George and Brookland Street Presbyterian church which was filled to overflowing.

Dr. Hugh Jack, pastor, conducted the simple but impressive service and assisting him was Dr. A. a. MacLeod of Sydney who led in prayer. Filled with pathos and drama was the rendition in Gaelic of the hymn, "Sweet Bye and Bye," by Mrs. Nevin Cameron of Sydney, an outstanding Gaelic singer. It was a particular favorite of the late Mr. MacIvor who was a deep lover of the music of the Gael.

Other hymns sung by the church choir were, "Onto the Hills" and "Jesus Saviour Pilot Me."

The eulogy of Dr. Jack was also simple. It touched upon his life as a student, Lawyer, and parliamentarian and the fair and efficient discharge of the duties entrusted to him.

The pastor reminded the gathering of the fact "his years of service were rendered under great difficulties ... due to physical application."

He Added; "He suffered more than most of us realized ... it was borne with great courage and without complaint."

The thousands who turned out to stand beside his bier in recent days was the greatest testimonial to his worth and character, the pastor stated.

A striking cross-section of provincial life was represented at the funeral service Friday night, and included the Masonic lodges in industrial Cape Breton, city police department, headed by Chief Vincent Campbell, the Cape Breton Barristers' Society. Nurses from the Victorian Order of Nurses and the Cape Breton division of the provincial department of health, County Court Judge George M. Morrison, Crown Prosecutor W. A. D. Gunn, O.C., C. B. county officials headed by Warden Ted Sullivan.

Others in the lineup were Michael MacDonald, CCP provincial leader John Macdonald, MLA, North Sydney, Robert Muir, MP, Sydney Mines, Innis MacLeod, Q.C., Halifax, representing the department of Premier Robert Stanfield; John A. Y. MacDonald, Q.C., and Henry F. Muggah, Q.C., representing the attorney-general's department; Earl Urquhart, MLA, M. A. Patterson, Q. C., prothonotary A. D. Muggah, county sheriff James MacKillop, county jailor Angus MacLeod.

Principal mourners and close associates occupied places in the centre auditorium. A wealth of floral offerings set off a picturesque backdrop for the oak casket in front of the chancel. Honorary pall bearers were; Donald C. MacNeil, MLA, representing the Hon. R. L. Stanfield, Premier of Nova Scotia; Mayor D. Owen Hartigan, Sydney Mines, president, Nova Scotia Liberal Association, representing Henry D. Hicks leader of the provincial Liberal opposition; provincial magistrate John F. MacDonald, Joseph G. Azar, Joseph Francis, Alfred E. Sibley, Robert Campbell, Dr. William Buchanan, representing the federal Liberal party; Sgt. Bill House, the RCMP.

Active pall bearers were: Donald MacLeod, Dr. Arthur W. Ormiston, Donald N. Nicholson, M. J. MacIvor, W. J. Stephens, and Stewart Stearns of Glace Bay. The remains were taken this morning at nine o'clock to Little Narrows where interment will be in the family plot in the Presbyterian church cemetery. Service at the church will begin at two o'clock in the afternoon.

Tyrian Youth Masonic Lodge, Glace Bay, of which Mr. MacIvor was a member, will conduct the committal service at the graveside. The Worshipful master of Tyrian Youth Lodge officiated at the masonic portion of the service in the church Friday night and will officiate in similar capacity at Little Narrows today.

Bibliography

Baker, Trudy. 2012. Various email interviews with the author. December 2012 – May 2013

Burgess, J.M. 1868. "Photography and Disease." Photographic News. Feb.-May, 1868.

Canada, Sessional Papers. 1892. "An 8 Act Respecting the Criminal Code," 55-56 V.

Christiano, Gregory. "The Blizzard of 1888; the Impact of this Devastating Storm on New York Transit." NYCSubway.org. http://www.nycsubway.org/wiki/The_Blizzard_of_1888;_the_Impact_of_this_Devastating_Storm_on_New_York_Transit (accessed June 26, 2013).
Duff, A.L. 1957. "The Trial Transcript of Dan Murdock Morrison," 1957.

Frazer, David. 1994. "History of the Upper Baddeck River Settlement." Reports: March 26, 1994. Beaton Institute. Cape Breton University.

Hirsch, Linda MacLean. 2013. Email to the author.

Haddad, Roger. 2013. (Retired RCMP Constable). Email to the author. May 16, 2013.

"Long Depression." 2013. http://en.wikipedia.org/wiki/Long_Depression (accessed May 16, 2013.

MacLeod, Roderick Angus. 1940. "Last Will and Testament," October 1, 1940. (Handwritten).Victoria County Land registry

McInnes, Joan. 1990. Victoria County Archives, June 16, 1990.
Morrison, Martha. 2013. Personal interview with the author. May 20, 2013.

Morrison, Shawna. 2013. Email interview with the author. May21, 2013.

Nova Scotia Archives and Records Management. 2013.

"Obituary of John (J.) Smith MacIvor." 1957. "Obituaries." Cape Breton Post. June 13, 1957.

Campbell, Peter A. and Ian Stott. 1981. "This Match Wasn't Made in Heaven," Cape Breton Highlander. Aug. 12, 1981. Killam Library Microfilm Collection, AN 5 C3 (accessed Feb. 2013). This includes all of the 7 part series through October 14, 1981.

Campbell, Peter A. and Ian Stott. 1981. "Daisy, Daisy, You're Driving Me Crazy," Cape Breton Highlander. Aug. 19, 1981. Killam Library Microfilm Collection, AN 5 C3 (accessed Feb. 2013)

146